Mysterious SIGNS Of The Torah Revealed In EXODUS

Dr. Akiva Gamliel Belk

Founder:

jewishpath.org

B'nai Noach Torah Institute, LLC

bnti.us

Copyright © 2013

Dr. Akiva Gamliel Belk

All rights reserved

ISBN-13: 978-0615750644

ISBN -10: 061570648

Publisher
B'nai Noach Torah Institute, LLC
Post Office Box 14
Cedar Hill, Missouri 63016
First Edition 2013

DEDICATED

Secret Acts!

To the one who meditates
In the Torah day and night...

To the one who cares about
being righteous and contrite...

To the one who understands
and cares for another's plight...

To the one who gives so others
may have pleasure and delight...

To the one whose love
is fashioned by The Torah's Light...

May the Lord God Bless You!

Mysteries SIGNS Of The Torah Revealed In EXODUS

Table of Contents

DEDICATED..5
FORWARD..9
PREFACE..13
ACKNOWLEDGEMENTS..15
GEMATRIA CHART..19
INTRODUCTION..21
   A New Ruler..29
Chapter 1..29
   One God...37
Chapter 2..37
   Remembering...53
Chapter 3..53
   Constancy..65
Chapter 4..65
  Yitro / Jethro's Name..75
Chapter 5..75
  Keeping His Commands Brings Blessings....81
Chapter 6..81
  Generously Give The Right Gift....................89
Chapter 7..89

Sanctified Clothing..101
Chapter 8...101
   Money Is Atonement...................................113
Chapter 9...113
   Aish / Fire..117
Chapter 10...117
   Everyone Is Important 123
Chapter 11...123
   Sanctifying Our Communication..................135
Chapter 12 135
About The Author...155

FORWARD

I have known many teachers over the years, some are well known, some are not. One thing I know about the author of this book is that he strives to live what he teaches. Dr. Akiva Gamliel has always required references for any work submitted to him. He follows those rules himself and documents all his work. This book is chocked full of information that most of us have never seen. In this book you will find pearls, nuggets of information, that up until this time have been left to Jewish scholars. For those who understand the many nuances of Hebrew, discovering these hidden treasures is easy. Yet I know it was not like this for Dr. Akiva Gamliel. At the age of 40, like the great Rabbi Akiva, he did not even know the Aleph Bet, i.e. the Hebrew Alphabet. He applied himself through study for many years. He speaks fondly of those days when he learned with 'his teachers' at the Rabbi's table at Yeshiva Toras Chaim during morning breakfast. Since those days Dr. Akiva Gamliel has grown a great deal. He would say, 'It's not enough'. During those years Dr. Akiva Gamliel began studying by invitation. He was invited to learn several evenings a week with a young Rabbi in an old old trailer in a cow field. Much has changed since then. The young Rabbi at that time was the Director of the Division of Community Services for Yeshiva Toras Chaim Outreach Center. Rabbi, Jacob Meyer is now the head Rabbi of Aish HaTorah, a large Orthodox Congregation and school in Greenwood Village, Colorado.

Back in those early days, Dr. Akiva Gamliel would learn 30 minutes each morning after prayers and before breakfast, with Rabbi David Nussbaum. He is a scholarly Bais Medrash Teacher at Yeshiva Toras Chaim. He is also the son in law of Rosh Ha Yeshiva's Rabbi Isaac Wasserman.

Dr. Akiva Gamliel learned with Rabbi Mordechai Twerski of the Orthodox Congregation Tri Sulom / The Resh Mem Kehilas Beis Yaakov and worked in the Pesach Matzah factory and as a moshgiach.

Dr. Akiva Gamliel also learned with Rabbi Israel Engel of Denver Chabad who is now the Rabbi of Bais Menachem in Denver and also the head of Colorado Chabad.

Dr. Akiva Gamliel's credentials are many. Besides authoring thousands of web pages on the study of the Torah he also teaches on a weekly basis to hundreds of students through out the world via the internet.

Most of us can use a little help peeling back the layers and uncovering the mysteries of Exodus. This book is for anyone who believes that the Torah is like an undiscovered country just waiting to be explored more deeply. As you read and study this book you will find truth if you are truly seeking it So let's begin this journey.

Brachah Rivkah Belk

PREFACE

This is the second book of The Mysterious SIGNS Of The Torah Revealed series. Five books are planned if God is Willing. The first book was entitled <u>Mysterious SIGNS Of The Torah Revealed In **GENESIS**</u>.

When writing this book, <u>Mysterious SIGNS Of The Torah Revealed In **EXODUS**</u> my goal was to first assign a chapter to each Parshat. (Many circles in Judaism use the term Parsha instead of Parshat.) In Judaism we study the Torah through out the year using different formulas. The most common form of study is by Parshat. Genesis has twelve Parshot, Exodus eleven Parshot, Leviticus ten Parshot, Numbers ten Parshot and Deuteronomy eleven Parshot. There are a total of fifty-four Parshot. Now, this formula would be easy to follow, except we have a few Holy Days, in which we emphasis the Holy Day instead of the Parshat. For example: the Festival of Tabernacles and the Festival of Passover. So all in all, there are normally more Parshot than Sabbaths during a lunar cycle. The exception is when we add an extra month. So, what I am saying is that, depending on the year you study using this book, it can vary a little.

Even though the Weekly Parshat tends to carry the message from one week to the next well, and normally follows chronologically, my style of writing is a bit eclectic. I like a book that has a variety of subjects. The point of reading a book with Gematria, is to learn something new, or perhaps, to gain a more thorough explanation of a subject that has never quiet made sense. I fancy searching the depths of Torah with a Gematria light, so to speak. It is exciting to discover a truth, like a nugget of gold deep within the earth.

Hermeneutically speaking, I believe that for every yes Gematria, there is a no Gematria. For every white Gematria, there is a Black Gematria. For every Gematria that pulls one toward there good inclination, there is a Gematria that pulls towards the evil inclination. Yet, having written this, ALL GEMATRIA MUST AGREE with the Torah's Message!

Dr. Akiva Gamliel Belk

ACKNOWLEDGEMENTS

My Momma set across the Sabbath table from me with large tears in her precious eyes. She was a frail lady with thick thick glasses. Her glasses were folded and lying on the table. Momma was unique in that she studied the Bible diligently. Of all the ladies I know, and have known Momma was idiosyncratic in that she righteously followed our Creator. When I reflect back over a half century of memories, it is a major challenge to think of one sin Momma may have committed. My Mother was a pillar of truthfulness. She was humble. She served others. Momma was patient. Momma was kind loving, caring and understanding. Momma was the perfect Mother.

Momma was sitting to my right, as she spoke of what troubled her. She felt like she needed to clear up a conversation of the past. The former conversation keenly upset her and she needed to clarify her position. Momma wanted me to understand that she was forced to agree to a phone message left by my father. Momma wanted me to know that she did not agree, and had been looking for the time when we could sit down to discuss the matter. We did. My Mother could not live with her self if she thought she had sinned. I have never seen anyone so profoundly moved by the possibility they may have committed a slight wrong.

As I grow older and closer to heavens door, I often return to thoughts of Momma. Momma is an example a paradigm, a righteous template, a prototype. I am trying to follow in Momma's footsteps. I want to reach her level before leaving this world.

Momma was nearly blind as heaven drew close. I remember Momma struggling to read from her Thompson Chain Large Print Bible with a magnifying glass. It hurt me so! She would tilt her head a certain way, then look out through her glasses and through the magnifying glass onto the Scripture lines.

Momma bought a large print typewriter. She would type out Bible Verses onto index cards to memorize. Momma memorized hundreds of Verses during her life. She tested herself daily. I receive a great deal of inspiration from Momma everyday. So dear Reader, this is one reason why we use 16 point type in this book. It is in honor of my mother, Mrs. Ethel, Anna [Channah] Horvat, Sakash Belk, may she rest in peace.

GEMATRIA CHART

Aleph	א	1			
Bet	ב	2			
Gimmel	ג	3			
Dalet	ד	4			
Hey	ה	5			
Vav	ו	6			
Zayin	ז	7			
Chet	ח	8			
Tet	ט	9			
Yud	י	10			
Chof	כ	20	Final	ך	500
Lamid	ל	30			
Mem	מ	40	Final	ם	600
Nun	נ	50	Final	ן	700
Samech	ס	60			
Ayin	ע	70			
Pey	פ	80	Final	ף	800
Tzzadi	צ	90		ץ	900
Quf	ק	100			
Reish	ר	200			
Shin	ש	300			
Tav	ת	400			

INTRODUCTION

Several decades ago I began writing portions of this book, <u>Mysteries SIGNS Of The Torah Revealed In EXODUS.</u> Through the pages are a blend of many years of study, Gematria compilation and gargantuan research. In preparing each of the eleven chapters I reviewed hundreds of pages of class discussions, notes and emails. It's unique to look for hour upon hour, even days, for a few lines that one remembers, and is fond of how they were written. I have done this often throughout these pages. They hold many memories for me. In chapter one I share the story of what a great leader Yoseif was, in comparison to the new leader, that would rule Egypt after his departure. Yoseif was so altruistic and philanthropic. He suffered a great deal and gave of himself. To get this message, one would need to have some background on Yoseif and what he had experienced. I did not retell the story. Who can tell a Bible story better than the Bible. No one! However I drew a stark contrast between Yoseif and the new ruler. I share a wonderful story of a well know Rabbi who exemplifies carrying. This story helps to deliver the message of Yoseif.

I use chapter two to drive home a message. My Father was very good at driving a message home. I learned from him. I share a discussion with my Rabbi, who has never heard the Voice of God. He is a good man. He is an excellent Rabbi. He is a great leader. He is a wonderful father and now a grandfather. Yet he has never heard the Voice of God. He was really reaching out to me. My Rabbi wanted to communicate how very very special it was for me to have heard God's Voice, just once. He longed to just share that experience. It was very special for me to hear the Voice of God. Well dear reader, I tried to make a bridge between this experience and a special revelation of God. The revelation is that God is One. Yet many will not be able to understand this because God has not revealed it to them. I make the point that many things will have to be revealed, and understood for our world to come together, under the coming Messiah. I go on for pages making my case knowing many will not be able to receive the revelation. Yet, it is there for them later, God Willing.

Chapter three is about remembering. We have a memory for a purpose. God often uses our memory to draw us to him. The point to chapter three is that one day, if we live a long life, we will be dried and used up. We will not be fresh and pliable. When we are young we may think that we will change when we get older. It may not be possible.

Chapter four is a contrast between the bitter waters of Marah and the sweetness of The Torah. I enjoy this discussion.

Chapter five is a discussion about the father-in-law of Moses, Yitro / Jethro. Many do not know that Yitro and Job were advisors to Pharaoh. Using Gematria I draw a line between Yitro and the Torah. Again some history really helps here. Few know of Yitro's righteous background. When he converted to Judaism, it was almost like, he came into Judaism at a higher level than Moses.

Chapter six is about how we are blessed through observing the Commands given to us by our Creator. For example the blessing of the Fifth Command, to honor one's parents is a longer life.

When one is young it may not seem important but when one is closer to heaven, it can become quite relevant. Using Gematria, I state, *When one observes the Laws of The Torah, the obedience to the Laws have a reward... they have a blessing.*

A story in chapter seven goes back over thirty years. It is about this old oak desk that some friends joined me in restoring. I cherished this desk. The memories surrounding the old oak desk were so warm and special. Yet I gave it away. I discuss the significance of what it is like, to give away, something one really values. This is a favorite chapter for me, in the book. I share a valuable principle about giving.

This is not about giving to plant seeds. It is not about sacrificial giving or giving till it hurts. There is a limit to giving, REGARDLESS of what any religious salesman is trying to sell. The is a story about the value of a gift. There are several great stories in this chapter.

The principle about giving the correct gift is crucial to living and being a blessed people.

I needed to write chapter eight. It provided an opportunity to speak out about an important message that NEEDS TO BE DISCUSSED!! It maybe a bit surprising. The chapter is heavy in places. I harp on a point we all need to get and get! Do we rid ourselves of communication devices? Are they evil? What should we do?

Atonement is the discussion in Chapter nine. This is another chapter that may require revelation. Many are taught an entirely different message about how one receives atonement. This discussion may seem out of bounds. However for those who will hang in there and who have a tender heart and want to really know the truth it is possible they may receive the revelation.

One can know the truth about atonement. And again, I really hammer a major theme home about separation. I hammer it so hard you may feel like you are bleeding. Yet, this is a crucial subject that really is extremely important!

Chapter 10 is about marriage. I love marriage. Marriage has not always loved me, Kaw Naw Nah Hah Raw. The Gematria lessons in this chapter are so soft and gentle and wonderful. Every individual needs to read this light chapter. One can learn so much from the Gematria principles surrounding marriage. We learn how God Created a man and a women. It is amazing! After you read this chapter you will KNOW it is the truth! God Bless you!

The final chapter just stops. However we stop with an important message. Everyone is important to God! I want each of us to know and feel our importance before God.

At times I will use a Jewish term followed by a forward slash defining the Word used. We are going to use this instead of a glossary. The first book in this series has a glossary.

Aleph to Tav - [א ת] When I use the words 'from Aleph to Tav,' I mean 'from the first Letter of the Aleph Bet, the Letter Aleph [א] to the last Letter of the Aleph Bet, the Letter Tav [ת].' The [את] Eht represents being all inclusive from the beginning of one letter to the conclusion of another letter. *'The word את Eht is spelled Alef Tav, the first and last letters of the Hebrew*

Alphabet. It therefore implies a transition from beginning to end. Rabbi Ishmael therefore states that its main purpose [in the instance he is referring to] is to indicate the transitive sense of the word "created."

Rabbi Akiba, on the other hand replies that the very fact that Eht contains the Alef Tav implies that it superimposes the entire alphabet between the subject verb and the predicated noun adding all things that pertain to that noun(Cf. Or Torah, Bereisheit). See <u>The Bahir</u> pp 108, 109

When I do this it is a bit awkward for the reader, yet necessary. It is unusual. Yet, it is really important. At the beginning of Chapter three the Aleph Tav is used three times in one Verse. This really defines how Pharaoh felt. It tells us Pharaoh was an absolute heathen. Without the use of Eht we would not see this.

Dear Reader, I am pleased with my book and truly believe it will make a very positive impression in your future. The principle are easy to understand. I believe my book will make a wonderful positive difference in your live.

A New Ruler
Chapter 1

Shemot
Exodus 1.1 – 6.1

Exodus 1. 8

וַיָּקָם מֶלֶךְ־חָדָשׁ עַל־מִצְרָיִם אֲשֶׁר לֹא־יָדַע אֶת־יוֹסֵף:

And He arose a new king to Egypt that did not know everything from Aleph to Tav of Yoseif.

וַיָּקָם
Vaw Yaw Kawm
And He Arose
156 = 40מ 100ק 10י 6ו

יוֹסֵף
Yoseif
156 = 80ף 60ס 10י 6ו

The Words מְצַוּךָ Mih Tzah Voo Chaw, meaning *Commanding You* and הָאָסִיף Haw Aw Seef, meaning *ingathering*. They are the Gematria 156.

מְצַוּךָ
Mih Tzah Voo Chaw
Commanding You
156 = 20ך 6ו 90צ 40מ

הָאָסִיף
Haw Aw See
ingathering
156 = 80ף 10י 60ס 1א 5ה

New leaders bring changes. Departing leaders

bring changes. With the departing of Yoseif / Joseph we see ingathering. With the new king we see commanding you…

In our world today we need ingathering that Yoseif brought. Yoseif brought families, peoples and nations together. Yoseif was concerned for all of The Lord's Creation. Notice the Final Letters of Yoseif and Haw Aw Seef. Both Words end in the Letter ף Final Pey. The Final Pey looks like a shepherd's staff. In our world we need people who care about others. We need the right type of leadership in every facet of life. We need leaders who draw people together. Our world is hurting for the right type of leadership. We see this in the Gematria 156. There are different types of people in leadership positions. One ף Final Pey the Verse the other concludes it.

Genesis 50.19 - 21
'Joseph said to them, Fear not; for am I in the place of God? But as for you, you thought evil against me; but God meant it to be good, to bring to pass, as it is this day, to save many people alive. Now therefore do not fear; I will nourish you, and your little ones. And he comforted them, and spoke

kindly to them...'

Many years ago as a staff member for a Jewish school I observed such an act. We were having the dedication for a new building. Great Rabbis were invited to participate from all around the country. The school was across the street from a major Hospital.

One afternoon during our celebration a young man came in the front door of the school heading right into the sanctuary where he sat down, bowed his head and remained quiet. He was from hundreds of miles away. I noticed him. One of the Rabbi's also noticed him. The Rabbi walked over to me, leaned over and whispered into my ear something like, *What does this young man need?*

My reply was, *I don't know.*

He immediately motioned for his assistance to go speak with the young man. Then he whispered another sentence in my ear, *'We should find out what he needs.'* This is what one expects of a great Rabbi. He was a Yoseif type leader.

We learned, the young man was Jewish. He lived in a small town hundreds of miles away. His wife was in the hospital having surgery. That Rabbi saw to it that this young mans needs were attended to.

We need rulers who care about people as this Rabbi did. The man was dressed in blue jeans. He was not wearing a kippah or tzitzit. So What! The keen sensitiveness of this great Rabbi has stuck with me.

Shemot 1. 8

וַיָּקָם מֶלֶךְ־חָדָשׁ עַל־מִצְרָיִם אֲשֶׁר לֹא־יָדַע אֶת־יוֹסֵף׃

And He arose, a new king to Mitzrim that did know everything from Aleph to Tav of Yoseif.

חָדָשׁ Chaw Dawsh, meaning *new* caught my attention. Chaw Dawsh also means *month*. The אֶת informs us the new ruler knew NOTHING of Yoseif's belief in God or anything about God. He did not know how to care for others like Yoseif did. He did not bother to find out! Caring does not necessarily mean giving other peoples money away. We find out what they need.

יָשַׁב Yoh Sayv means *settled in* or to *begin dwelling.* When the new ruler dwelt in the land of Egypt he brought new drastic changes. The Gematria for חָדָשׁ Haw Dawsh [Chadesh] and the Gematria for יָשַׁב Yoo Sayv are both 312.

חָדָשׁ
Haw Dawsh
New
312 = 300ש 4ד 8ח

יָשַׁב
Yoo Sayv
Settle In
312 = 2ב 300ש 10י

In Yoseif's hand we see the shepherd's staff. In the new ruler hand we see the masters whip. We continue discussing the Letter Pey which we began with Exodus 1.8. The Letter Pey is associated with speaking. As already noted

Yoseif spoke words of comfort while the New Pharaoh spoke words of pain.

Exodus 1.9 – 12
[Pharaoh] said to his people, Behold, the people of the children of Israel are more and mightier than we; Come on, let us deal wisely with them; lest they multiply, and it may come to pass, that, when there would be any war, they should join our enemies, and fight against us; and so get them out of the land. Therefore they did set over them taskmasters to afflict them with their burdens. And they built for Pharaoh treasure cities, Pithom and Raamses. But the more they afflicted them, the more they multiplied and grew. And they were mortified because of the people of Israel.'

Let's bring this discussion to the 21st century. I am **DISPLEASED** with the disingenuous way Senators, Congressmen and politicians vote!! We the people have said to them we need a budget for you to follow. The budget must lower our over all debt. We must spend less this fiscal cycle than in the previous fiscal cycle. One must question, are they interested in what we need?

One God
Chapter 2

Va'eira
Exodus - 6.2 - 9.35

Exodus 6.2

וַיֹּאמֶר יְהֹוָה אֶל־מֹשֶׁה עַתָּה תִרְאֶה אֲשֶׁר אֶעֱשֶׂה לְפַרְעֹה כִּי בְיָד חֲזָקָה יְשַׁלְּחֵם וּבְיָד חֲזָקָה יְגָרְשֵׁם מֵאַרְצוֹ׃

And The Lord Said to Moses, soon you will see what [I will do to] Pharaoh. For with [My] strong hand [he will] send them out and with a strong hand he will drive them out of his land.

Exodus 6.3

וַיְדַבֵּר אֱלֹהִים אֶל־מֹשֶׁה וַיֹּאמֶר אֵלָיו אֲנִי יְהֹוָה׃

And He, God Spoke to Moses, And He Said to him, I am The Lord.

Exodus 6.4

וָאֵרָא אֶל־אַבְרָהָם אֶל־יִצְחָק וְאֶל־יַעֲקֹב בְּאֵל שַׁדָּי וּשְׁמִי יְהוָה לֹא **נוֹדַעְתִּי** לָהֶם :

And [I] Appeared to Abraham, to Jacob and to Issac as God Almighty and not by My Name The Lord. [I] did not **reveal** *to them.*

The Word נוֹדַעְתִּי Noh Dah Tee means 'reveal'. The Gematria of נוֹדַעְתִּי Noh Dah Tee is 540

נוֹדַעְתִּי
Noh Dah Tee
נ 50 ו 6 ד 4 ע 70 ת 400 י 10 = 540

שָׁמַר
Shaw Mahr
To Guard
ש 300 מ 40 ר 200 = 540

A revelation from God is very special. We must carefully guard revelations. We have to be careful not to loose what we have. We have to be careful to keep the rust off the revelations the Creator Gives us. His revelations are precious to us. My Rabbi once spoke to me. He said, '*Akiva, do you know how fortunate you are? You have heard the Voice of God at least four times. I have never heard the Voice of God. I envy you!! You are truly Blessed!*' He is right!

Dear Reader the Torah portion of the Bible was given to Moses by the Voice of God. The Torah is a revelation of God! No other Book of the Bible was spoken to the Writer Word for Word. In this chapter we are going to review how God [singular] Spoke these Words.

The Name אֱלֹהִים El Loh Heem is plural. אֱלֹהִים means gods when it is not used in reference to God as Judge or Creator. Even though the Name אֱלֹהִים El Loh Heem is plural אֱלֹהִים El Loh Heem is <u>ALWAYS</u> used as singular when reference is made to God as Creator. Why? אֱלֹהִים El Loh Heem our Creator is One. The Name אֱלֹהִים is singular in Exodus 6,3. The Name אֱלֹהִים is always used with the singular intent when used in reference to God.

Christians are taught that God is three in one.

Christians believe God is a trinity. They believe that God Shares His power as Father, son and Holy Spirit. This teaching is not correct. God is only One. God is A Spirit. God is Creator. In Judaism we call God our Father. We say אבינו מלכנו, meaning Our Father Our King even though the Words אבינו מלכנו do not appear anywhere in Ha Tenach [the Hebrew Scriptures]. We do this because we see God as Creator. As Creator of everything we refer to God as 'Father.' God is Father of everything. However when we refer to God as Father we are NOT SAYING that God is two separate beings or two beings in One. We speak affectionately of God as being our Father because God is our Creator.

Unfortunately there are those who have allowed themselves to be misled by our affectionate use of referring to God as our Father. Our intent was NEVER to imply that God had a son. We recognize that it is IMPOSSIBLE for God to have a son.

However this confusion is understandable to us. Our Creator chooses to reveal Himself differently between various groups. Remember what our

Creator Said,

Exodus 6.4

And [I] Appeared to Abraham, to Jacob and to Issac as God Almighty and not by My Name The Lord. [I] did not reveal to them.

No matter how much we teach and share that God is ONLY ONE some may not receive this because God has not revealed it to them. They are following God with the light He has provided them. So no matter how much I want others to understand that God is Not three in One until the Creator reveals this to them they will not understand.

When one wants to formulate a doctrine they search for a place that they maybe able to formulate that doctrine. This is what happened with Christianity. Hundreds of years ago Catholic leaders searched for a place to formulate a doctrine that God is three in one. *'The First Council of Nicaea was a council of Christian bishops convened in Nicaea in Bithynia* [This is present-day Iznik in Turkey. Today Turkey is Islam. 99 percent of the population is registered as Islam.] *by the Roman Emperor, Constantine I in 4,85 From Creation, i.e. 325 CE. The Council was historically significant as the first effort to attain consensus in the church through an assembly representing all of Christendom.*

The First Council of Nicaea is generally regarded as having been the first Ecumenical Council of the Christian Church. Most significantly, it resulted in the first uniform Christian Doctrine called the Creed of Nicaea. The purpose of the council was to resolve disagreements arising from within the Church of Alexandria over the nature of Jesus in relationship to the Father; in particular, whether Jesus was the literal son of God or was he a figurative son...'

This is where the doctrine of the trinity originated. This doctrine is incorrectly based on Genesis 1.26. Why? There appears to be a crack in the wall that could be taken advantage of.

Genesis 1.26

וַיֹּאמֶר אֱלֹהִים נַעֲשֶׂה אָדָם בְּצַלְמֵנוּ
כִּדְמוּתֵנוּ וְיִרְדּוּ בִדְגַת הַיָּם וּבְעוֹף
הַשָּׁמַיִם וּבַבְּהֵמָה וּבְכָל־הָאָרֶץ וּבְכָל־
הָרֶמֶשׂ הָרֹמֵשׂ עַל־הָאָרֶץ׃

And He Said [singular] Elohim / God [plural] Make Adam in our image [plural] in our likeness [plural] and let them rule [plural] fish in the waters and birds in the heavens and with all animals in the earth and with all creeping on the earth.

We know that God is Spirit. Christians teach this. The Christian Scriptures say,

John 4:24
God is a Spirit *and they that worship Him must worship Him in Spirit and in Truth.*

Hebrews 1:7
And of the Angels He Says, ***'Who makes His Angels Spirits*** *and His Ministers a flame of fire?*

Why do I mention this? In Genesis 1.26 God Whose Form is Spirit Spoke to Angels whose forms are Spirit. <u>This was NOT God as Father Speaking to Jesus as son</u>! Let's examine Genesis 1.26 with the proper intent.

And He, Elohim / God Said [to the Angels. Let us] Make Adam in our [Spiritual] image in our [Spiritual] likeness and let them [Adam and Eve] rule fish in the waters and birds in the heavens and with all animals in the earth and with all creeping on the earth.

What actually happened. Note the next Verse.

Genesis 1.27

וַיִּבְרָא אֱלֹהִים אֶת־הָאָדָם בְּצַלְמוֹ
בְּצֶלֶם אֱלֹהִים בָּרָא אֹתוֹ זָכָר וּנְקֵבָה
בָּרָא אֹתָם:

And He, [singular] God [plural] ***Created*** *[singular] everything from the Letter Aleph to the Letter Tav of the man [singular] in His Form [singular]. In His Form [singular] God [plural] Created them [plural] male and female, He Created them [plural].*

What is the point? In Genesis 1.26 God Was Speaking to the Angels. God Could have been Speaking to anyone or anything. The proof is in Genesis 1.27. The proof is in what God actually did. God is 'ONE' and God Who's Name Elohim is Plural Created singular in His Form singular and in His Image singular… This is what God Did. Lets examine.

Form - Look at the Letters carefully.
Genesis 1.26 - בְּצַלְמֵנוּ - Plural - In our Image / Form – Strong's # 6754
Genesis 1.27 - בְּצַלְמוֹ - Singular - In His Image - The Complete Hebrew English Dictionary

Likeness
Genesis 1.26 כִּדְמוּתֵנוּ - Plural - In our Likeness Strong's #1823

Genesis 1.27 - בְּצֶלֶם - Singular - In His Form - see Strong's #2183 The Complete Hebrew English Dictionary

Please ask questions. Judaism has nothing to hide. The fact is that God who is One, not three in one, Created Adam the first man and Eve, the first woman in His Form.

Dear Ones we have a body. Our body came from the dust. Each of us has a Spirit. Our Spirit may also be called our Soul or our Mind. The misuse of these terms gives the appearance that we are three in one. Our Body houses our Spirit. It's that simple. We were Created in God's Spiritual Form.

Bereisheit / Genesis 2.7

וַיִּיצֶר יְהֹוָה אֱלֹהִים אֶת־הָאָדָם
עָפָר מִן־הָאֲדָמָה וַיִּפַּח
בְּאַפָּיו נִשְׁמַת חַיִּים וַיְהִי
הָאָדָם לְנֶפֶשׁ חַיָּה׃

And He [singular] The Lord [singular] God [Plural - used as singular] Formed [singular] everything from Aleph to Tav of Ha Adam / Adam and Eve from dust of the ground and He [singular] blew into the nostrils the Soul of Live and it happened Ha Adam / The Man became a living Soul.

What is the point?

There is no evidence that God is three in one. This Verse refers to The Lord God in the singular. Adam and Eve were Created as living Souls / Spirits. This is what the Bible Teaches.

In this Verse we noted that the Words יְהוָה אֱלֹהִים The Lord God are used together. The combination of the Words יְהוָה אֱלֹהִים The Lord God are scribed dozens of times together through out Scripture. EVERY TIME they are written together they are written in the singular. They are NEVER used in the plural form.

We began this discussion with Exodus 6.2 - 4. I want to return to this discussion now. Why? Exodus 6.3 clearly makes the point that the word אֱלֹהִים Elohim / God is singular. Let's observe.

Exodus 6.3

וַיְדַבֵּר אֱלֹהִים אֶל־מֹשֶׁה וַיֹּאמֶר אֵלָיו אֲנִי יְהוָה

And He [singular] God [plural] Spoke [singular] to Moses. And He said [singular] to him. ***I am*** [singular] ***The Lord*** [singular].

וַיְדַבֵּר

Vah Yih Dah Bayr, meaning, *'And His Word'*, is singular. Whose Word, in this Verse, is reference made to? This Verse is making reference to the Word of God. Not the Words of gods. The fact is that He or His is singular. He or His does not make reference to more than one.

וַיְדַבֵּר אֱלֹהִים

Elohim meaning gods or judges that is unless אֱלֹהִים is in reference to God who is One. Why is it that the translators of the Bible translate אֱלֹהִים as God? I acknowledge that the Word אֱלֹהִים is plural. Since אֱלֹהִים is plural why not translate אֱלֹהִים as gods?

In the beginning Gods created the heaven and the earth. And the earth was without form, and void; and darkness was upon the face of the deep. And a wind from Gods moved upon the face of the waters. And Gods said, Let there be light; and there was light. And Gods saw the light, that it was good; and Gods divided the light from the darkness. And Gods called the light Day, and the darkness he called Night. And there was evening and there was morning, one day.

What is the point?
The point is that it is WRONG to say that the Word אֱלֹהִים in Genesis 1.26 refers to Gods, i.e the trinity and to not carry this same theme through the rest of the Bible. The fact is that Christian Scholars understand the intent is God and not gods.

And He [singular] the Word [singular] Elohim / God [used in the singular].

אֶל־מֹשֶׁה
To Moses

וַיֹּאמֶר
And He [referring to God Who is written as plural and referred to here in the singular] Said. Why is this written, He Said? Why doesn't it say, 'They Said'? Christian cannot have it both ways.

וַיֹּאמְרוּ
'They Said.' If God was intended to be plural this is what would have been written.

אֵלָיו
To him [Moses]

אֲנִי
Anh Nee, meaning 'I' is singular. I, Who Am referred to as אֱלֹהִים – Am The Lord. In this Verse we see God Saying I am The Lord. We note that Elohim Refers to Himself in the singular, as 'I'. It is incorrect to claim God is three in one!!

יְהֹוָה
HaShem / The Lord [Am singular].

Exodus 6.4
וָאֵרָא אֶל־אַבְרָהָם אֶל־יִצְחָק וְאֶל־יַעֲקֹב בְּאֵל שַׁדָּי וּשְׁמִי יְהֹוָה לֹא נוֹדַעְתִּי לָהֶם:

And [I Spiritually] Appeared [singular] to Abraham, to Jacob and to Issac as God [singular] Almighty [singular] and by My Name [singular] The Lord [I] [singular] did not reveal to them. Then the following Verse follows with how God Revealed Himself to Abraham, Jacob and Issac.

Again, No matter how much we teach and share that God is ONLY ONE if God has not revealed it to you then you may not understand.

I encourage those who hunger to know the Truth learn Hebrew.

With over 730 religions and 35,000 splinters off these religions has anyone questioned, how will Messiah draw all the people of differences together. Revelation is the answer. With less than the blink of one eye God can eliminate all confusion. We will see clearly. Areas we cannot understand today can be clarified in less than one eye flash. It is very very likely many living today will see this in this life. I am saying Moshiach / Messiah is not far from coming. Today, we are living in the closest time to Messiah coming than at anytime in the past.

Remembering
Chapter 3

Bo
Exodus 10:1 – 13:16

Exodus 5:2

וַיֹּאמֶר פַּרְעֹה מִי יְהוָה אֲשֶׁר אֶשְׁמַע בְּקֹלוֹ לְשַׁלַּח אֶת־יִשְׂרָאֵל לֹא יָדַעְתִּי אֶת־יְהוָה וְגַם אֶת־יִשְׂרָאֵל לֹא אֲשַׁלֵּחַ:

And He, Pharaoh said, Who is The Lord that I should listen to His Voice, to let everything from the Letter Aleph to the Letter Tav of Israel go? I do not know [anything] from the Letter Aleph to the Letter Tav [about] The Lord, nor will I let [anything] from the Letter Aleph to the Letter Tav of Israel go.

Pharaoh was steeped in hard denial. Not only was he unwilling to acknowledge his sin of oppressing B'nei Israel, he increased the level of oppression. Pharaoh also denied the existence of God.

Throughout this parshat we are constantly reminded that Pharaoh's heart was hard, that his heart remained set in preventing B'nei Israel from worshipping The Lord! His denial was a public denial! It was a sin against The Lord and against His people. B'nei Israel!

He ordered his officers to afflict B'nei Israel! At each turn in the course of events, The Lord Tells Moses to remind Pharaoh and the people of Egypt.

'...that I am The Lord...' Exodus 7:5

'By this you will know that I am The Lord...' Exodus 7:17

'...You will know that there is none like The Lord, our G-d..' Exodus 8:6

'...You will know that I am The Lord in the midst of the earth...' Exodus 8:18

'This is what The Lord the God of the Hebrews has said...' Exodus 9:1

'...so that you may KNOW that there is none like Me in all the earth.' Exodus 9:14

'...so that My Name will be declared throughout the earth.' Exodus 9:16

Long before this point, the end of the fifth plague, Pharaoh knew! Yet, he continued in his ways of sinful disobedience of The Lord's Commands. There are those who know what The Lord has Commanded yet in outright denial they continue in their pattern of sin. Their conclusion will be like that of Pharaoh and Egypt. They will cross the line as Pharaoh did. Pharaoh reached a place where he was no longer was able to control his own heart... his thoughts... his actions... The Torah tells us that God took control of them. **God**

hardened his heart! When Pharaoh had a choice he chose to oppress B'nei Israel. He chose to continue in his pattern of disobedience. He chose to continue his denial of The Lord. He crossed the line that no one should cross. He could not return. This is the danger of the one hardened in denial of The Lord and His Commands!!

Holy reader, a staff member at JewishPath posed this question: Can't a Jew return from wherever they are, from however far they have fallen? Isn't the Jewish light an eternal light? Well, the answer is Yes and No! Yes in the sense that it is possible. Yes in the sense that The Lord can draw anyone to him. However in the practical sense, No! Don't be fooled! When a tree is young it is flexible but when it is old the flexibility is gone. If it bends too much it will break. This should serve as a caution to us not to live on the outer perimeters of Judaism where God forbid, one's lifestyle may prevent one from repentance...

One may think that eventually they may change their mind, BUT that is not necessarily true. Those like Pharaoh, who cross the line, or those who live on the outer perimeters may go to far. It is a very scary, dangerous place to dangle with one's life! I don't like this type of teeter.

When I was a child my Father, may he rest in peace, would give an illustration to the children at youth camp. He had a bundle of sticks that were smooth and dried out. He picked these sticks up along a beach in the San Francisco Area. He also had several freshly cut Aspen branches. Daddy showed the children how flexible the young Aspen branches were. He would bend them in every direction with out breaking a branch. He show how stiff and how unforgiving the smooth dried sticks, he found along the ocean were. He could not bend them at all. Daddy made the comparison. Daddy explained that when we are young we can go in many directions. Then he taught, when we are older, we will be hardened. We will not be able to go in many directions. He explained that now was the time to let God shape our lives. Then, again reminding us many years later it would be difficult, and possible impossible, because we would be to set in out ways.

When I read this story of Pharaoh I thought of this story Daddy told. Now, in this week's parshat we read, The Lord Said to Moses, *'Go to Pharaoh for I have made his heart stubborn and the heart of his servants...* [Why?]*...for the purpose of establishing a sign of these [great miracles that I performed] amidst [B'nei Israel]. And for the [explicit] purpose that you [carefully] recount [these great miracles] in the ears of your children and your children's children, [especially] how I made a mockery of Egypt with great signs and how I ostracized them that you know that I am The Lord.'* Exodus 10:1,2

The words Voo Li Mah Yahn - Ti Sah Payr, meaning " for the [explicit] purpose that you [carefully] recount [these great miracles]..." so that you may relate... so that you may tell your children and your children's children... This is Jewish 'T R A D I T I O N'! Holy reader, telling ... carefully recounting... is a very important Mitzvah / Command, yet there is another crucial point to this story. That point is, can a individual cross the line? Can a individual reach a place where there is no point of return? Where

REPENTANCE does not exist? Certainly Pharaoh reached this point! We clearly observe this time and again when The Lord Hardens his heart. {See Exodus 9:12, 10:20, 10:27, 11:10 and 14:8}.

וּלְמַעַן תְּסַפֵּר
Voo Li Mah Yahn - Ti Sah Payr {Gematria Motel}

וּלְמַעַן
Voo Li Mah Yahn {and to relate}
וּ6   ל30   מ40   ע70   ן50 = 196

תְּסַפֵּר
Ti Sah Payr {to recount [like in a book]}
ת400   ס60   פ80   ר200 = 740

Total
945 = 196 + 740

Now when we read the words Vah Yi Chah Zayk - The Lord - Eht - Layv - Pharaoh, meaning *'And The Lord stiffened everything from Aleph to Tav of Pharaoh's heart....'* We understand that Pharaoh could NOT choose to let B'nei Israel go. Letting B'nei Israel go was not among his options. **Pharaoh's heart was stiffened like it was written in a book** because The Lord wanted to make a point with Egypt - "JUDGMENT"- and at the same time establish an unforgettable sign with B'nei Israel through His great miracles of deliverance.

Genesis 15. 13,14

And he said to Abram, Know for a certainty that your seed shall be a stranger in a land that is not theirs, and shall serve them; and they shall afflict them four hundred years; **And** *also* **that nation, whom they shall serve, will I judge;** *and afterward shall they come out with great wealth.*

The Lord desired to establish a Jewish tradition centering around our deliverance from Egypt by His great acts. While at the same time, He pronounced Judgment on Egypt for the years B'nei Israel suffered under their cruel and harsh treatment!!

So, holy reader, we can see the point of deliverance, but what about the point of crossing the line. Can we see it? When we look into the Gematria we can observe the cautions of not going too far, of being careful, of not wandering beyond voice distance or we may get lost... When our children were young we would go camping, fishing and hiking. I had one serious rule that everyone had to follow, 'Don't get out of sight or voice range!'

This past year a young child was hiking with friends. The child disappeared and has not been seen since.

Dear reader, when considering the question, Can a Jew reach a place where there is no point of return... a place where REPENTANCE does not exist?... I prefer to address that question by asking, Why live on the edge... why teeter on some distant fringe?? To me it is frightening to even think of living near the edge... Why risk it? Why come in just under the line? Why graduate with low marks? Why? We see the connection in the Gematria of 945 with the words:

וַיְחַזֵּק יְהוָה אֶת־לֵב פַּרְעֹה
Vah Yi Chah Zayk - Lord - Eht - Layv – Pharaoh

וַיְחַזֵּק
Vah Yi Chah Zayk {and He stiffened}
131= 100ק 7ז 8ח 10י 6ו

יְהוָה
Lord
26 =

אֶת
Eht {from Aleph to Tav – meaning everything}
401 = 400ת 1א

Layv {heart}

32 = 2ב 30ל

פַּרְעֹה

Pharaoh {King of Egypt}

355 = 5ה 70ע 200ר 80פ

Total

945 = 131 + 26 + 401 + 32 + 355

Dear Reader, on the one hand we are to recount the great miracles that The Lord performed in punishing Egypt while delivering B'nei Israel / The Children of Israel. And on the other hand we are to remember the warning of living on the edge.. of living a non repentant life... of denying The Lord's existence... of pleading ignorance to who The Lord is! Dear one, now is the time to move closer to an observant life!!

We are reminded that everything we do is recorded in a book of Remembering.

I pray that each of us will be blessed with the desire to live an observant life and that we will be able to influence other Jews to move away from the assimilated edges towards Torah Judaism. May The Lord bless each of us!!

For those who are not Jewish but want to be Jewish... Or perhaps you have reason to think you are from one of the lost tribes... Or possibly feel like you are Jewish but don't know... Or you have relatives who are Jewish... Or you know nothing about Judaism or Jewish Observances... I encourage you to read my book, Would You Like To Be Jewish? My goal is not to convert you but help you find answers.

In this chapter I wrote to those who are Jewish. Yet, many of the questions I asked Jews in this chapter also apply to B'nai Noach / non Jews. In the concluding chapter of this book I discuss how import each of us are to our Creator.

Constancy
Chapter 4

Beshalach
Exodus 13:17 – 17:16

Exodus 15.22

וַיַּסַּע מֹשֶׁה אֶת־יִשְׂרָאֵל מִיַּם־סוּף וַיֵּצְאוּ אֶל־מִדְבַּר־שׁוּר וַיֵּלְכוּ שְׁלֹשֶׁת־יָמִים בַּמִּדְבָּר וְלֹא־מָצְאוּ מָיִם׃

So Moses brought everything from Aleph to Tav of Yisrael from the Sea of Reeds, and they went out into the wilderness of Shur; and they went three days in the wilderness, and found no water.

וַיָּבֹאוּ מָרָתָה וְלֹא יָכְלוּ לִשְׁתֹּת מַיִם מִמָּרָה כִּי מָרִים הֵם עַל־כֵּן קָרָא־שְׁמָהּ מָרָה׃

Exodus 15.23

And when they came to Marah, they could not drink of the waters of Marah, for they were bitter; therefore its name was called Marah.

They came to Marah expecting one thing but got another. The intention of B'nei Israel was to find water, what they got was bitter water.

The Gematria for Marah is 245.

מָרָה
Bitter
245 = 5ה 200ר 40מ

מהר
Moh Hahr
Contract price, to hurry,
245 = 200ר 5ה 40מ

Hah Mayr
המר
Change
245 = 200ר 40מ 5ה

Dear ones, it is so easy to get caught up in the emotion of the minute. B'nei Israel just experienced the greatest military victory of their lives. The greatest, most feared army of Egypt had just been annihilated. They watched as the waters came crashing down on horse, chariot and rider. They observed as foot soldier, sergeant and captain drowned in the Yam Suf / the Reed Sea. They saw their once feared tormenters eliminated in an instant, never to bother them again. Under such circumstances it is extremely difficult not to get caught up in the singing and rejoicing. After all, this was a very great victory. This was a powerful deliverance by The Lord.

The same can be said for tragedy. On the morning of 9-11 I was preparing to leave for work when the phone rang. The caller was our son. He stated, "Turn on your television, Avie. The World Trade Center has just been hit by a terrorist plane." I turned on the television and watched. Soon my ride to work arrived at the door. He came in. I asked if he had heard the news. He said, "What news?" I invited him to join me. We sat their stunned as the events of the day unfolded. We decided to not go to work that day. We watched for hours....

Holy reader, it is easy to get caught up in festivities and in tragedies. We must be careful.

While we need to rejoice and mourn we must still remain constant in our observance of Torah study. If we allow ourselves to be drawn away or permit ourselves to be attracted to something other than what it is we should be doing, we may be endangering our own existence. This is what happened to B'nei Israel in Parshat Beshalach. This is what can and occasionally may happen to us. We must be careful.

In all the rejoicing, B'nei Israel neglected to study The Torah for three days. Their neglect immediately resulted in the evaporation of their entire water supply. B'nei Israel went for three days without water and without studying The Torah. Their rejoicing almost immediately turned into tragedy. Over three million people were in need of water. The mothers, children and fathers needed water. Millions of sheep and cattle needed water. The vast herds grew weak. Everyone was searching for water. No one could find water. Things were quickly becoming desperate.

The point is being constant in times of rejoicing and tragedy. The point is remaining constant in all types of weather. **This is why our Sages instituted the reading of Torah on Shabbat, Monday and Thursday so B'nei Israel would never again go three days without Torah study.** You see we became so involved in a good thing... a great deliverance... a great victory... a powerful miracle that we neglected a very important thing, our Torah study.

So even though there are times that by accident or need we are drawn away from our important responsibilities of studying Torah, during each day our sages have placed a guard... a fence... a protection in our path to protect us from the bitter waters. That guard is consistency. It is good to rise at the same time each day. It is good to study at the same time each day. It is good to pray at the same time each day. In other words, it is important to develop a life built on consistency. I refer to this as digging a rut. When a Jew has deep ruts to follow throughout life it is much easier. There is nothing wrong in hugging deep ruts. They keep us consistent. They keep up us in place, God Willing, the right place. What I am saying is that for the observant Jew there is always a place that we are supposed to be and normally that is good. The problem erupts when we get out of our rut. Emergencies, vacations, meetings all have the potential of drawing us away from where we are supposed to be and away from what we should be doing. As an author of parshat studies each week, I must carefully guard my time. Studying, preparation and writing require many hours each week. I spend hours at work each week and driving between home and work. Each day begins with prayer. The night normally concludes with supper before bedtime and prayer. The days are long. The nights are short. Every minute of the day is scheduled in some form.

Dear Reader it does not matter how high one can climb. One can fall just as far. These principles are not for you alone but for me also. They are for all of us. One of the guards or fences the Rabbis strongly encourage is living in a Jewish Community. I did not use the word Orthodox for a purpose. Live next door to Jews. Live across the street from Jews. Live down the block from Jews. I appreciate the wisdom of living in a community. Several of the great mistakes in my life have been living outside the Jewish

Community. Choose a community that is large enough to allow for some privacy. Choose a community with choices of many congregations. If it is not possible to live in a community then associate closely with the community. Attend studies, events, social gatherings daily prayer and Sabbath services when possible. Remember the waters of Marah were bitter but Ha Torah is sweet.

Psalms 19.8 – 12
The Torah of the Lord is perfect, reviving the soul; the testimony of the Lord is sure, making wise the simple. The statutes of the Lord are right, rejoicing the heart; the commandment of the Lord is pure, enlightening the eyes. The fear of the Lord is clean, enduring for ever; the judgments of the Lord are true and righteous altogether. More to be desired are they than gold, even very fine gold; sweeter also than honey and the honeycomb. Moreover by them is your servant warned; and in keeping of them there is great reward.

If we make the right changes we can avoid a lot of bitterness.

One Sabbath, while camping near Triangle Circle, about 26 miles up in the mountains above New Castle, Colorado, several family members took a hike. It was intended to be a short hike. We could not carry. It did not turn out that way. We refers to this hike as the Nine Mile Hike. We do not know how long it actually was. However, hours later by the time we found our way back to camp we were very thirsty.

I saw this water bottle lying there. I was very thirsty. I picked it up and removed the cap. I began to drink. I rinsed my mouth. After a couple of gulps I spit the rest out. PHEW!! Have you ever opened a plastic water bottle that has been sitting in the sun for a long time? Not only is it hot but it has a horrible taste. I can only imagine what it was like for B'nei Yisroel after traveling three days without water and then to see this wonderful looking oasis with what appeared to be refreshing water. Can you imagine bending down to drink this water? Can you imagine how awful the water tasted. B'nei Yisroel could not drink the water because it was so bitter.

We allowed our good intended walk to take us

away from where we need to be. We allowed our walk to place us in a difficult place.

A friend from the Jewish Community stopped by my place of employment. During our brief conversation he asked, "Akiva, what day do you have off?" I responded, "Truthfully, only Shabbat!"

Dear ones, I remember the words of a Teacher who studied with me. He said something to the effect of, 'Akiva, there is never a time for a Jew to let his hair down. We are always suppose to be aware of God's Presence.' A Jew should always be somewhere. That somewhere is planned. That somewhere is prepared. That somewhere is deliberate. Unfortunately, B'nei Israel allowed themselves to be drawn out of that consistent cycle that my teacher spoke of. We must guard our constancy. May The Lord bless us with being great rut huggers!

We must be careful to fill our cups with The Torah several times a week. We must stay true to our agreements. Our actions God Willing will keep our water delightful...

Yitro / Jethro's Name
Chapter 5

Yitro
Exodus 18.1 – 20.23

Exodus 18.1

וַיִּשְׁמַע **יִתְרוֹ** כֹהֵן מִדְיָן חֹתֵן מֹשֶׁה
אֵת כָּל־אֲשֶׁר עָשָׂה אֱלֹהִים לְמֹשֶׁה
וּלְיִשְׂרָאֵל עַמּוֹ כִּי־הוֹצִיא יְהוָה
אֶת־יִשְׂרָאֵל מִמִּצְרָיִם:

When **Yitro / Jethro**, the priest of Midian, Moses' father-in-law, heard of all that God had done for Moses, and for Israel his people, and that the Lord had brought everything from the Letter Aleph to the Letter Tav of Israel out of Egypt...

Our sages say that Parshat Yitro was added in honor of Moses's father-in-law. This parshat was named after Yitro. It expresses his wisdom and powerful contribution to our system of justice in the Torah. Yitro was a man who understood government, politics and justice. He was Priest of Midian. He was a consultant to Pharaoh. And then he was an advisor to Moses our teacher. Yitro was a convert to Judaism. He was a spiritual leader of Midian. It is for these reasons and others that this week's Parshat was named after him. In fact within our Torah there are only a few Parshot named after people: Noach, Chayei Sarah, Yitro, Korach, Balak and Pinchas. As a result we should begin to sense how very special Yitro is.

We are informed that Yitro had seven names: Re'uel, Yesser, Yitro, Chovev, Chever, Keini and Putiel.

Yeter: meaning abundance, surplus, excess. It was from the essence of this name that "Yeter" made a powerful contribution to the Torah. We see a special connection to his gift in the Gematria of his name.

Yeter
610 = 200 ר 400 ת 10 י

Yeter is a relative to the Gematria 609 and 611. The Gematria 611 represents "Torah".

Torah
611= 5 ה 200 ר 6 ו 400 ת

This is significant because it tells us how close Yeter lived to the Torah before his conversion. It is also special because the letter ו Vav was added to his name. The letter ו Vav is a connecting letter in our language. It connects letters, words, sentences, paragraphs, thoughts, etc. Here the letter Vav represents a connection from Yeter to Yitro to the Torah! The ו Vav also represents a connection that a non Jew makes when he / she converts to Judaism. The non Jew receives a Hebrew name. The letter ו Vav is added to Yeter after his conversion thus becoming Yitro. In other words, it is somewhat comparable to adding the letter ה Hey to Torah. When we add the letter ה Hey to Torah it represents an article. So Torah becomes "The Torah." We now compare the Gematria of Yitro with "The Torah." Both are the Gematria 616.

Yitro
616 = 6 ו 200 ר 400 ת 10 י

Torah
616 = 5 ה 200 ר 6 ו 400 ת 5 ה

The Gematria 616 expresses the full acceptance of "The Torah" by Yitro. who after his full acceptance of "The Torah" How fitting for the man who contributed to our system of justice in The Torah!

In addition to this, the Gematria 616 is 'MYSTICAL' in the sense that it represents acceleration, the increase, the uplifting of one's day. We see this in the Gematria Godal of Yom, meaning 'Day'. The normal Gematria of day is 56 but when we use the Gematria Miluy Godal, we so to speak elevate the day, i.e the normal Gematria transcends to Gematria Godal 616! Our day takes on a 'GREATNESS'. Can one think of a higher form of elevation than the day one converts or returns to Torah observance?

Yom {day}
40 ם 6 ו 10 י

Yom {day} Gematria Godal
616 = 600 ם 6 ו 10 י

One should notice the symbolic place that Parshat Yitro begins, Chapter 18 representing חי Chai {"LIFE"}... that is, the new life of Yitro!

חי
Chai - Life
18 = 10 י 8 ה

Holy reader, B'nei Israel had fallen to the 49th level while they were captives in Egypt. They were only one level from the very lowest level. They almost reached the place where they may have crossed the line that we spoke entitled Remembering. Our Sages Say there were three reasons they did not fall to the lowest level which may have prevented their return. One of those reasons was that they kept their Hebrew names. They used their Hebrew identity! It is our Hebrew Name that has essence. It is our Hebrew Name that is scribed in the book of Life.

Keeping His Commands Brings Blessings
Chapter 6

Parshat Mishmash
Exodus 21.1 – 24.18

Exodus 21.1

וְאֵלֶּה הַמִּשְׁפָּטִים אֲשֶׁר
תָּשִׂים לִפְנֵיהֶם :

And these, the Laws that set before them.

Dear Ones a while back I had the special opportunity to visit a new congregation which is just a few months old. This is the second time Revi and I visited. The first time we visited a man in the Congregation gave us his Chumash / The Five Book of Moses. Chumash means five. At that time the Congregation did not own any Chumashim. This touched us. As a result B'nai Noach Torah Institute gave 14 full size Stone Chumashim to the Congregation from our Seforim Fund.

Last Shabbat we visited again. It was good to see the Seforim in use.

This Congregation was a split off another local congregation. I attempted to bring the two groups together. Both groups were challenging. They eventually worked through their differences. The end results were that wounds were healed and they came back together. However, at the time I wrote this Parshat they were still divided.

At that time I wrote a number of Letters, spoke on the phone with each group and invited both groups to our home to discuss the matter. These were very special individuals with different ideas about what was best for the congregation. The division was a great deal about the future of the congregation. There was a load of love and pain on both sides. Thank God over time differences were worked out. Individuals were trying from many sides to help. Eventually several leaders from each group were able to span broken bridges, encourage trust and issues began to get resolved.

On one of those snowy days I took my lunch break to visit their Sunday School It was wonderful. There were classes for the infant / preschool children up through adult. Scattered throughout the study room in the home were the Chumashim. What a blessing.

During the visit it was a privilege to spend about ten minutes in two classes and about twenty in another. A board member informed me that the older children were making a Book on Rabbi Akiva. The books were about 18" wide and 24" long. This is a great lesson for all involved. The love and work placed into the home spun books will last for years and be used by many younger children. They are being assembled with much attention to detail. I was impressed. Rabbi Akiva was the great Torah Sage I wrote of in the Dedication of <u>Gematria And Mysticism IN Genesis.</u>

In another class the Teacher informed the students that this Parshat had the most Mitzvot of all the Parshat in Ha Torah. She used several vivid examples to convey an important meaning to her students. She told the students, that what they already possess, is worth more than if they won a great deal of money from the lottery... and she brought her point home with more examples...

The infant / preschool children were joined by several parents. It is especially pleasing to see parents involved taking an interest in their child's education. When the parent is involved it tells the child the message is important. The children were learning the Aleph Bet and saying the names of different clothing in Hebrew.

Dear Ones it was real good to see this start up congregation in action. It was even better when all the differences were worked out between the two groups and everyone united in Love.

This brings to the forefront an important message. When ever congregations do not agree, or families do not agree, or husbands and wives do not agree Ha Torah still requires obedience and conformity. There is great reward in obedience!!

God Willing we are going to examine the Mysticism of Shemot 21.1.

וְאֵלֶּה הַמִּשְׁפָּטִים אֲשֶׁר תָּשִׂים לִפְנֵיהֶם :

And these, the Laws that are set before them.

The Sages Say it's like preparing a banquet of many excellent foods that will entice one to eat. The purpose of learning these Laws is to Observe them.

וְאֵלֶּה
Vih Ay Lehh - And These
6 ו 1 א 30 ל 5 ה = 42

הַמִּשְׁפָּטִים
Ha Meesh Paw Teem
The Laws / Judgments
ה 5מ 40ש 300פ 80ט 9י 10ם 40 = 484

Total
42 + 484 = 526

These are the Laws that came to our father Abraham in a Vision.

Genesis 15.1

אַחַר ׀ הַדְּבָרִים הָאֵלֶּה הָיָה דְבַר־יְהוָה
אֶל־אַבְרָם בַּמַּחֲזֶה לֵאמֹר אַל־תִּירָא
אַבְרָם אָנֹכִי מָגֵן לָךְ
שְׂכָרְךָ הַרְבֵּה מְאֹד:

Genesis 15.1

After these things **the word of the Lord came to Abram** *in a Vision, saying, Fear not, Abram; I am your shield, and your reward will be great.*

הָיָה דְבַר־יְהֹוָה אֶל־אַבְרָם
the word of the Lord came to Abram
20 = 5 ה 10 י 5 ה
206 = 200 ר 2 ב 4 ד
26 =
31 = 30 ל 1 א
243 = 40 ם 200 ר 2 ב 1 א
Total is 20 + 206 + 26 + 31 + 243 = 526

When one observes the Laws of Ha Torah the obedience to the Laws have a reward... They have a blessing.

וַאֲבָרְכָה מְבָרְכֶיךָ
Vah Ah Vaw Rih Chaw
Mih Vaw Rah Cheh Chaw
And I will Bless from Your Blessing
234 = 5 ה 20 כ 200 ר 2 ב 1 א 6 ו
292 = 20 ך 10 י 20 כ 200 ר 2 ב 40 מ
Total is 234 + 292 = 526

מוֹפֵת
Moh Fayt
means sign or miracle
526 = 400 ת 80 פ 6 ו 40 מ

Deuteronomy 7.9
Know therefore that The Lord your God, He is God, the faithful God, which keeps the covenant and mercy with those who love Him and keep His Commandments to a thousand generations; And repays those who hate Him to their face, to destroy them; He will not be slack to him who hates Him, he will repay him to his face. You shall therefore keep the Commandments, and the Statutes, and the Judgments, which I Command you this day, to do them.

Remember what we discussed in Chapter five.
Psalms 19.8 – 12
The Torah of the Lord is perfect, reviving the soul; the testimony of the Lord is sure, making wise the simple. The statutes of the Lord are right, rejoicing the heart; the commandment of the Lord is pure, enlightening the eyes. The fear of the Lord is clean, enduring for ever; the judgments of the Lord are true and righteous altogether. More to be desired are they than gold, even very fine gold; sweeter also than honey and the honeycomb. Moreover by them is your servant warned; *and in keeping of them there is great reward.*

Generously Give The Right Gift
Chapter 7

Terumah
{Exodus 25:1 - 27:19}

Exodus 25.1 – 8
And the Lord spoke to Moses, saying, Speak to the people of Israel, that they bring me an offering; from every man that gives it willingly with his heart you shall take my offering. And this is the offering which you shall take from them; gold, and silver, and bronze, And blue, and purple, and scarlet, and fine linen, and goats' hair, And rams' skins dyed red, and goats' skins, and shittim wood, Oil for the light, spices for the anointing oil, and for sweet incense, Onyx stones, and stones to be set on the ephod, and on the breastplate. And let them make me a sanctuary; that I may dwell among them.

Some years ago several rabbium, and I founded and operated a non profit program. We solicited new and used gifts from our community. The organization gave the gifts to Jewish educational institutions that needed them, sold others gifts to raise funds for Jewish education and discarded the unusables. We were paid for bulk clothing and shoes etc. One day we were having a yard sale. Many items were on display, including a dozen or so bikes in very rough condition. A middle aged man seemed to be taking an interest in these bikes. A few of us noticed. We thought maybe he was a bike dealer. After a while I approached him to begin a conversation. The first words out of his mouth were, *'It's amazing what junk some people will give to a non profit organization.'*

Over the years I have experienced and shared many humorous and sad stories. I cannot count the times someone has said to me, *'Akiva, it's amazing the discards people try to pawn off on non profits.'*

Dear reader, We would receive calls. The giver

would describe the item over the phone. Their description would sound like ice cream with chocolate syrup melting down the sides, with nuts scattered generously over it with a cherry on top. We couldn't wait to receive the contribution. Well, needless to say, it did not take us long to begin asking several questions like, How old is it? Does it have any rips, tears, holes, worn spots, stains? What color is it? Does it need cleaning? With televisions, radios, stereos, refrigerators, ranges, etc. we would ask does it work... properly...?

Even after this, on some occasions when we would arrive to receive the contribution you would think we spoke a different language. I recall the conversation with an individual after refusing to accept her contribution. She was sincere. This professional blew big time. She said, 'What's the matter with you? I can't believe this! We took this furniture out of our home. It was good enough for us! The board of your organization is going to hear about this! Leave it! I'll call the Salvation Army.' I made the mistake of saying, "They won't take it either..."

Her contribution was a particle board computer desk from Noah's ark. It had a hole in the side the size of a football. The children had redecorated it with paints and stickers. Unfortunately I touched it and it fell over. There were other items but...

I cannot count the shoes with holes, the high heels without the heel, the pants where the seat was missing, the faded dresses, the stained shirts and blouses, pots and pans without handles, etc.

Actually we did receive many very good usable gifts but our focus today is on acceptable gifts. Many gifts were not acceptable.

Years ago I purchased an old oak desk that several friends help restore to its original condition. This took much work. It was drenched in white and blue enamel paint. We spent days of stripping, sanding, oiling, etc. This desk lived in my study at home. At my office I had a new solid wood executive desk. It was nice but I like the old oak desk the best. When the office was closed I had two desks. A friend expressed a desire for my old restored oak desk. I did not want to part with it. I gave it to her and her husband even though it was very special to me. Years later when my friends no longer required the desk they gave it back to me.

It is one thing to give away a useless piece of discarded junk and an entirely different matter to give away a priceless, warm, special treasure that happily lives in your home or office.

This week's parshat is saying only certain things belong in God's House. Only certain chosen items can live in the Mishkon. Other items cannot connect or attach to what is designated as Holy, as Separated for the Mishkon and its purpose and its service.

Now this is a problem for some of us. We struggle understanding the designation of HOLY or SEPARATED! In Judaism we have many categories that The Lord has said are Holy and that The Lord has Separated. It is unfortunate when we fail to comprehend the elevated status of these items. In Judaism we take certain mundane items, things, articles, clothing, seforim, places, animals, birds, fish, people; and we separate them and bless them. These items become Holy! They become Sanctified to The Lord.

Our Sefer Torah is written by hand, Letter by Letter on parchment / kosher animal skins, with a feather quill from a kosher bird. A Sofer / a Scribe, a very holy man who daily visits the mikvah for ritual cleansing, writes the Sefer Torah.

Not just anyone can write a Sefer Torah. Not just any parchment will do. Every quill is not acceptable. In the same way with gifts. Every gift is not acceptable. **This mentality of... 'Because we're giving it away it should be accepted' is wrong!** I was told of the story about A rabbi of a struggling girls' high school on the east coast of America. He refused a contribution that many would have jumped at. It was a lot of money! This Rabbi understood the meaning of separation. He didn't look the other way as so many have done. I was told he refused the gift because of the lifestyle of the contributor. He made a statement about real Judaism. Baruch HaShem! May God

Bless him and others who do the same.

We are suppose to have a standard in Judaism. The Lord is the architect, the general contractor, the purchasing agent, the builder and the inspector. He determines how things are done. This week's parshat relates the material for the construction of the Mishkon along with the exact construction details.

At jewishpath.org we receive correspondence from people who are frustrated, angry, confused and so forth. Some seem to write their own religious beliefs! Some seem to be selecting the parts of this religion that they like and parts of that religion that they like, etc. One cannot do that in Judaism! For some reason there are individuals that think they can observe Judaism and other religions. Some people believe they can properly observe Chanukah and Christmas, Pesach and Easter or Shavuot and Pentecost.

The point is, ONLY CERTAIN MATERIALS are usable in the Mishkon. PERIOD! These materials were selected by God! They are the only ones that can be used! In Judaism things are done a certain way. Judaism is NOT one of these flexible mix and match kinds of religions! The same God who said ONLY THESE ITEMS CAN BE USED IN THE CONSTRUCTION OF THE MISHKON IS THE SAME GOD WHO DEFINED JUDAISM!

God set a standard for Jews to live by and that is what we had better do! If we want God to live in our house then it has to have the material that God has prescribed. It has to be built according to God's directions. God will not live in a house built with unsanctified materials. God will not live in a house constructed in a way other than He has directed. This is one of many reasons why intermarriage is SO VERY WRONG FOR THE JEW! It's a mix and match of materials! God cannot sanctify the relationship! IT IS WRONG!

There was an individual who was employed to work on a particular project. He was the purchasing agent for this project. His responsibility was to acquire the material according to the required specifications. Years later that structure developed problems. An investigation was made. The investigator determined that the purchasing agent ordered an inferior product, a product not acceptable according to the required specifications. This man was terminated from that company and held responsible for his actions. Why is it that we can understand this, but we cannot understand God's instruction?

There was another man who was a general contractor on a project. He was responsible for building a custom home. He modified a room from the original plans by just six inches without telling anyone. He saved thousands of dollars because of his modification. This modification was not discovered until the owners were moving in. Their grand piano would not properly fit in its designated area. Why? A special area, a balcony overlooking the front room lounge designed just for this very expensive and impressive piano was modified. Can you imagine the frustration? Can you imagine the problem? The custom home was perfect except for... Years went into the planning and now...

Dear reader, God has made a plan that He expects to be followed. Our junky discards are unusable and unacceptable. God requires men and women with a GENEROUS HEART, people who will follow His instructions. God wants people who will not attempt any substitutions or modifications. Modifications by men and women will NOT WORK in God's plan. Otherwise they are no longer God's Plans.

Dear Reader this was a problem for Cain, the son of Adam and Eve. He brought spoiled flax seed as an offering. His offering was rejected. He was angry with God because his offering was rejected. Is this what we want? Rabbi Meir Zlotowitz and Rabbi Nosson Scherman, <u>The Artscroll Tanach Series - Bereishis Vol. I(a)</u> (Brooklyn, New York: Mesorah Publications, Ltd. 3rd Impression, 1989), p 144

תְּרוּמָה
Terumah means donation, a portion set aside
ת400 ר200 ו6 מ40 ה5 = 651

Terumah – With the Terumah we cannot give away everything. – We can only a portion. God's Command to contribute to building the Mishkan even precedes His Command to actually build the Mishkan.

Each gift that was brought to build the Mishkan elevated this world. Each gift of myself that I bring to The Lord elevates a *spark* of creation.

Silver was used to build the framework of the Mishkan. Silver as we all know has dross and has to be refined. So we refine the silver. We remove the impurities. It must be done His way. We want a Mishkan that is useable. We want a Mishkan where He can and will Dwell.

אִמְרָתִי
Ee Mih Raw Tee = Listen to my words
651 = 10י 400ת 200ר 40מ 1א

When we do want we want who is in charge? This is perhaps like following one of the many religions in the world. Our goal should be to obey the Commands of the Creator and to stop listening to the religions of the world.

Giving with a GENEROUS HEART is important. Giving a useable gift is also very important. God has specified what He can use. What does God need from us?

Sanctified Clothing
Chapter 8

Tezaveh
Exodus 27.20 – 30.10

Exodus 28.3

וְאַתָּה תְּדַבֵּר אֶל־כָּל־חַכְמֵי־לֵב אֲשֶׁר
מִלֵּאתִיו רוּחַ חָכְמָה וְעָשׂוּ אֶת־בִּגְדֵי
אַהֲרֹן לְקַדְּשׁוֹ לְכַהֲנוֹ־לִי

And you speak to all wise of heart Them that are completely filled with the Spirit of Wisdom *And they shall make* everything from Aleph to Tav of the clothes for Aaron To sanctify [to serve] as a Priest to Me.

Shemot / Exodus 19.6

וְאַתֶּם תִּהְיוּ־לִי מַמְלֶכֶת כֹּהֲנִים
וְגוֹי קָדוֹשׁ אֵלֶּה הַדְּבָרִים אֲשֶׁר
תְּדַבֵּר אֶל־בְּנֵי יִשְׂרָאֵל׃1

And you shall be to Me a Kingdom of *Priests* And a sanctified nation These are the Words that you shall say to B'nei Israel.

The purpose for comparing is to point out that just as the Kohan Gadol and the Kohanim are sanctified through clothing as stated in Shemot 28.3 so is every Jew because we are a kingdom of Priests to the entire world. There are several points to consider.

First is that Kal Israel is sanctified through clothing just as the Kohan Gadol and the Kohanim are. Our sanctified clothing is different from theirs.

Second is the concept of making sanctified clothing. Ha Torah Says, *'And they shall make everything from Aleph to Tav of the clothes for Aaron'*. What does this mean? It means there is a plan, a pattern to follow and there is a goal. How does this apply to us? Are we to wear clothing like the Kohan Gadol or the Kohanim? What is the point?

The point is clothing is sanctified. Marriage is sanctified. Israel is sanctified. The Kohanim are sanctified. The Kohan Gadol is sanctified. **Each of these are sanctified through clothing.** One of the keys is 'speak to all wise of heart'. **It is**

important to have direction with the clothes we cover ourselves with. Another point is that **ONLY those who are completely filled with the Spirit of Wisdom can be selected to make this sanctified clothing.** Making sanctified clothing require Chochmah / Wisdom and being over flowing with the Spirit of Wisdom… How many clothing designers and manufactures meet these requirements? Why are these important requirements?

Think about the importance of making Holy / Sanctified clothing. Only few have the wisdom to qualify. Why is wisdom so important? It is because those of us who are not as enlightened may make the wrong pattern or may select the wrong material. Remember we are forbidden to mix Shaatines, i.e. mix wool and linen within the same garment…

Wisdom, insight, sound learning are required to Teach Kal / All Israel about the holiness of clothing. Those who are wise of heart understand the reasons why covering the body is necessary. They also know what parts of the body require covering. I am not in this category, i.e. those who are wise of heart regarding with regards to clothing. Why? I have many questions that need answering regarding clothing. This being the situation, I do not have sufficient wisdom to explain some of the finer details in a fashion that other will understand and accept.

Why Jewish men should wear a Kippah and women should not...
Why Jewish men should wear a Tallit with Tzitzit and women should not...
Why our Sages Teach ladies should follow the custom of wearing a head covering... What types of head coverings...
Why our Sages Teach ladies should not wear mens clothing... What is the definition of men's clothing?

There is a point. I think the wise of heart can discuss and fully answer all questions regarding these issues. The Wise of heart are 'OVERFLOWING' with all that is necessary to answer our questions in these areas. Their answers are compelling.

Some of us follow the instruction of our Sages

without understanding the purpose other object to the observance because they do not consider the information they have been provided is compelling enough. For some it is necessary to have all of their questions answered before they take on an Observance. They want to know the ins and outs of the Observance before taking it on. This is not how we acted when receiving Ha Torah. Still it can be challenging for one to Observe a Mitzvah based solely on an incomplete Teaching... This is why it is good to ask questions and to learn all the answers....

Having said all this we even when we do not understand a Mitzvah we are not released from observing it...

In the Sefirot, the emanation Chochmah / Wisdom is an emanation shared more by women than by men. Yet, women are and have been prevented from learning many books of the Sages. Women have been omitted from being a member of the Bet Din, the Jewish court and from being part of the Sanhedrin. How do we explain this?

Clothing is a material thing with a Spiritual purpose. When HaTorah Says these are the clothes you shall make we can begin to understand material things are sanctified for holy purposes...

Exodus 28.4
And these, the Clothes that he shall make:
Breast plate
and a Eiphod
and a robe
and a checkered undershirt
a turban
a sash-belt
And make sanctified garments For Aharon you brother And for the sons to serve Me as Priests.

Exodus 31.10
And everything from Aleph to Tav of the clothing of the service And everything from Aleph to Tav of the sanctified clothing for Aharon the Priest And everything from Aleph to Tav of the clothing the sons for Priests

Shemot / Exodus 28.5
And he, Moses went down from the

Mountain To the people [B'nei Israel] And sanctified everything from Aleph to Tav of the people And they immersed [themselves] and their clothing

Bereisheit / Genesis 35.2
And Jacob said to his household And to all the people with him Get rid of everything from Aleph to Tav of these the foreign gods in your midst Purify yourselves and change your garments.

Yisaiah / Isaiah 61.3
To appoint to them that mourn in Tzion To give to them Beauty instead of dust / ashes Oil for Joy instead of mourning The Garment Mantel of Praise instead of the spirit of heaviness And to call themselves Leaders of the Righteousness who are planted by The Lord for Beauty / Glory.

בֶּגֶד Beged, meaning Garment has the exact same letters as בָּגַד bagad, meaning to betray, to deceive. The difference is how clothing is designed and how clothing is worn.

My wife Brachah Rivkah says,

There is a physical function of clothing and a spiritual function of clothing.

Clothing can be a distraction.

Clothing is intended to be Spiritual.

Our clothes show how we Honor and Glorify The Lord.

Our clothing communicates messages to the world.

What message am I sending?

Marriage Clothing
A wife gives her husband a Tallit to wear during prayers this is a special sign that to many means he is married. This depends upon the custom. However the point is he covers himself with the cloth garment his wife has prepared or purchased for him. He secludes himself within the Tallit. He communes with the Creator within the Tallit. It is like the tallit is a garment that wraps around their marriage.

Adam and Chavah were enwrapped by the Glory of our Creator. This means they were in the center of Tiferet / Beauty. Adam was not on the left and Chavah was not on the right. They were in the exact center. This is the Spiritual place for marriage. This is correct. Spiritual attraction is the greatest. Physical attraction may draw us to an individual. Spiritual attraction is what keeps spouses engaged and in love with each other. Adam and Chavah were in the center of God's Glory. When they departed the center of God Glory is when each sinned. When they sinned they were outside of Tiferet...

The clothing of the kohanim and kohen gadol are called begadim.

The kohen gadol's primary function was to provide atonement. Each piece of his clothing provided atonement for specific sins. [See Exodus 28.4]

Only Aaron's garments are composed of blue, purple, scarlet, gold and twined thread. These are the same materials that comprise the curtains of the Mishkan.

On the Kohen Gadol's forehead was a plate engraved saying Holy to the Almighty. Ramban Says that the commandment to dress the High Priest in garments for glory (*kavod*) and splendor (*tiferet*) is not only to enhance the status of the priest himself, but also to enhance the Glory of God.

לְכַהֲנוֹ־לִי
Lee Chah Hah No – Lee – To Be A Priest to Me To Serve Me
151 = 10 י   30 ל   6 ו   50 נ   5 ה   20 ב   30 ל

אָקִים
Aw Keem - I will Establish
151 = ם 10 י 100 ק 1 א

These Words are rare. לְכַהֲנוֹ־לִי Lee Chah Hah No – Lee, – To Be A Priest to Me To Serve Me occurs only three times in the Torah Portion of the Bible. אָקִים Aw Keem, - I will Establish occurs only twice in the Torah portion of the Bible. In the first, לְכַהֲנוֹ־לִי our Creator is Saying the office of High Priest is for the purpose of serving Me. In the second Word, אָקִים the

Creator 'Established' the Covenant with Yitzchok / Isaac and the Office of Prophet. This shows us how very very carefully our Creator selects and uses Words. Here we have several Words that are used for a combination of just five times in the Torah portion of the Bible. These Words share a Gematria relationship of 151. We see the significance and the exclusivity knowing that Lee Chah Hah No – Lee, – is in reference to the Kohan Gadol, the High Priest. There is only one High Priest at a time. We realize the clothing that was made that we discussed in this chapter was for him only. And we realize that his service was to the Creator of the universe exclusively. Then we see the priests of Israel and Israel as the priests to the world. Each of these are rare. Each of these are special. How do we act? Do we think of ourselves as being Priests to the World? Our clothing should reflect our uniqueness. Everything about us should reflect our uniqueness!! ...and we should be humble and meek even though we are most unique.

Money Is Atonement
Chapter 9

Ki Tisa
Exodus 30.11 - 34.35

Exodus 30:11

וַיְדַבֵּר יְהוָה אֶל־מֹשֶׁה לֵּאמֹר:

Exodus 30:11
And The Lord Said to Moses, Saying,

Exodus 30:12

כִּי תִשָּׂא אֶת־רֹאשׁ בְּנֵי־יִשְׂרָאֵל
לִפְקֻדֵיהֶם וְנָתְנוּ אִישׁ כֹּפֶר נַפְשׁוֹ
לַיהוָה בִּפְקֹד אֹתָם וְלֹא־יִהְיֶה
בָהֶם נֶגֶף בִּפְקֹד אֹתָם: יג

Exodus 30:12
Take a head count of everything from Aleph to Tav of B'nei Israel to determine the amount each **man** shall give as an **atonement pledge** for his soul to The Lord when you count them and as a result there will be no plague among them when you count them.

We want to center on the Words אִישׁ כֹּפֶר Eesh Coh Fehr, meaning Man's Atonement Pledge. Man's Atonement Pledge is represented by a half shekel coin for each man above the age of twenty. Each man brought a half shekel as an atonement for his soul. אִישׁ כֹּפֶר Eesh Coh Fehr, is the Gematria of 611. The Gematria for תּוֹרָה Torah / Law, meaning the 613 Commands of Ha Torah of the Law is also 611. This tells us that obeying, i.e. observing the 613 Commands of Ha Torah is and atonement for our soul.

תּוֹרָה
Torah / Law, meaning the 613 Commands of Ha Torah of the Law.
611 = ת400 ו6 ר200 ה5

אִישׁ כֹּפֶר
Eesh Coh Fehr
means - Man's Atonement Pledge
611 = א1 י10 שׁ300   כ20 פ80 ר200

When man follows Ha Torah, Ha Torah atones for man. How do we know this? The Gematrias are the same. The Torah is Perfect. The Torah can and does atone for man. So in the Observance of Torah we see atonement for man.

May each of us be Blessed with the atonement of Torah.

Aish / Fire
Chapter 10

Vayakhel
Shemot 35.1 - 40.38

Exodus 35.3

לֹא־תְבַעֲרוּ אֵשׁ בְּכֹל מֹשְׁבֹתֵיכֶם בְּיוֹם הַשַּׁבָּת :

Exodus 35.3
You shall not kindle fire in any of your dwelling places on the Sabbath day.

Fire is both a representation of man's technological mastery and as a symbol of man and Woman's emotional drives

Individuals must practice how to control their technological advances as we will discuss in Chapter twelve. There we will discuss controlling our technological advances. In this chapter we want to focus of individual responsibilities of controlling emotions, and desires and how it is accomplished through marriage.

An individual that is single is not benefiting from the lessons of marriage. Marriage is a union between a man and a woman. Marriage is called 'Holy Matrimony'. The man is separated to his wife and the wife is separated to her husband. NOTHING is suppose to come between them all the days of their lives, Kaw Naw Nah Haw Raw!!

The goal of 'Holy Matrimony' is to learn how to live in peace and harmony with another individual that is the opposite of you. Both learn to share. Both learn how to cooperate. Both learn how to function as a unit. Both learn how to successfully raise children together. Both learn how to worship together. Both learn how to observe Sabbath and Holy Days together. Then there are the relative issues. They are complex also. Both learn how to get along with their spouses relatives. Husband and wife do this their entire lives while living near a very hot bed, FIRE! Remember the old saying, Don't play with FIRE? Remember old Smoky the bear? Only you can prevent Forest Fires!

In marriage relationships a אִישׁ husband has his own FIRE and a אִשָּׁה wife has her own FIRE.

אִשׁ

The Letter Yud i.e. the center Letter for אִישׁ meaning man represents strength. The Letter Yud is the first Letter of the Lord's Holy Name. The Lord Placed the Letter Yud between the Aleph and The Shin so man would have the possibility of peace and happiness. The Letter Yud stands next to the Letter Hey. The Letter Yud represents the Ten Commandments that expand out to all 613 Commands of the Torah. Man is suppose to follow the Commands that pertain to him. In addition the Letter Yud represents strength, the Gevurah of man. Man is supposed to use his strength wisely, i.e. to keep the Letter Aleph and the Letter Shin apart. Use the Yud to prevent fire. Otherwise there is fire. God, please help us. It takes a real man to use the Letter Yud wisely to avoid hot burning fire.. God Assist us please. Man was designed to walk a tight line. Man was designed to walk on egg shells.

אִשָׁה

The Letter Hey diffuses the fire… The Letter Hey controls the fire. The Letter Hey is the second Letter in the Holy Name of the Lord. The Letter Hey stands next to the Letter Yud. The Letter Hey is represents the Five Books of the Torah. Inside the Five Books are the 613 Commands. The wife is required to follow the Commands that pertain to her. So to speak, the fire has to pass through the Divine Space, i.e the 613 Commands, the Five Books.. In other words the fire is calmed and supervised with kindness when it passes through the Letter Hey, Divine Supervision. The fire is tempered. A wife was designed to walk on a tight wire. A wife was designed to walk on egg shells.

Dear Reader this is how our Creator designed the man and the woman. Good relationships learn how to avoid fire while having plenty of warmth for comfort. We have this potential for fire but we don't have to have fire.

The Letter Aleph represents God's Name. The Letter Aleph represents one thousand. The Letter Aleph is the first Letter for both אִישׁ Man and אִשָּׁה Woman. When the Letter Aleph is spelled out the Gematria is 111. This tell us God is 1. God is 1. God is 1.

The Letter Shin שָׁלוֹם means peace. The Letter Shin also represents שַׁדַּי The Almighty One. Before one enters their home or their bedroom a Mezuzah is attached to the door frame. On the Mezuzah are the Letters reminding the Husband and wife שַׁדַּי The Almighty One. When the Letter Shin is spelled out the Gematria is 360. This tells us that the relationship between a husband and wife needs to be a complete circle. There are no corners. This represents the eternal relationship of their marriage. When the Aleph (111) and the Shin (360)_ are joined side by side properly they combine to represent מְלֵאת Mih Lay Oot meaning Complete or Fullness.

מְלֵאת
Mih Lay Oot
means Complete or Fullness.
471 = 400ת 1א 30ל 40מ

אֶלֶף
Aleph
One or One Thousand – Represents God
111 = 80ף 30ל 1א

שִׁין
Shin
The Almighty One
360 = 50ן 10י 300שׁ

Total 111 + 360 = 111 + 360 = 471

Husband and wife are only complete and full with each being in proper balance.

Everyone Is Important
Chapter 11

Pekudei
Exodus 38:21 - 40:38

In the parshat this week, our attention is drawn to those who are not the planners of the Mishkon or the contractors or even the laborers. Yet, they are there. They are very important and their contribution is also important.

Frequently we receive mail from readers. Ocassionally a reader writes about feeling left out because they are not Jewish. And as a result, God Willing, I am writing two Books which will soon be released. One is entitled <u>Would You Like To Be Jewish</u> and the other is entitled <u>God's Plan From the Beginning</u>. I am excited! Kaw Naw Nah Hah Raw!

On one occasion a lady wrote in an E-mail that even the gentiles are God's Children and that God Created them also. This is certainly true. The world we live in does have many members and many religions. Her note was an excellent reminder for to be considerate, mindful and careful of others. We are not to blind ourselves of our neighbors or their important contribution. Yet, one should understand that jewishpath.org, jewishpath.com and jewishlink.net are Jewish websites with the goal of assisting those who are Jewish. However we also have bnti.us - B'nai Noach Torah Institute, LLC and 7commands.com which are designed for everyone to be a part.

In this Parshat we learn that the offerings given to build the Mishkon were requested of B'nei Israel, the Nation of the Covenant. These were offerings were from people who were commanded to be 'Shomar Sabbath', meaning people who guard the Sabbath. This they sanctified the Sabbath. They set aside Sabbath as Commanded in the Torah. They did their work on the other six days. Now it was from these people that The Lord commanded Moses to request the Terumah offering. What that meant was that God wanted the Mishkon, His future dwelling place, to be built from contributions by His people, B'nei Israel, who were separated from the rest of the world, who were living in the Bamidbar under His immediate direction. That does not imply that the rest of the world is not important. Yet, on the other hand, it does draw a very straight line.

There is a difference between Jewish beliefs and beliefs of other 730 religions with some 35,000 splinter religions of the present world. In Judaism we, the Jewish people, are Commanded by God to follow the Torah. Many of us do but many do not. In the Torah, Gentiles are commanded by God to observe a portion of the Torah, I.e. the Seven Commandments which expand into many more Commands. Some observe these Commands and other do not know they exist.

Now if you're building a house, who do you want to build it? Do you want people who are observant to your Commandments or people who don't know they exist? Do you want people who identify with your ideology or people who object? Do you want people who live Judaism second by second or people who are acquainted with it? The issue here is simple, God chose B'nei Israel to build his Mishkon because they were separated to Him.

Originally God offered His Torah to the other sixty-nine nations of the world. They rejected His Torah. Only Kal Israel wholeheartedly accepted The Lord's Torah. So why would The Lord include nations that rejected Him in the building of his Mishkon?

Dear Reader, the fact is that you and many besides you want to be Jewish is for a reason. You relate to the Commands. You relate to the call. Chances are you will convert. Chances are you will be Jewish. Chances are you were called from before the beginning to be Jewish.

On the other hand, the fact is that often Jews feel somewhat left out, too. We are not the Levium who work in close contact with the Mishkon or the coming Beit Ha Mikdosh. We do not set it up or take it down. We do not work in the courtyards. Yet the fact is that even the Levium who have this close contact may also feel somewhat left out because the Kohanim are the ones who offer the blessings, light the Menorah and offer sacrifices. Yet the Kohanim could feel a little left out because only one of them can be the Kohen Godal, the High Priest.

My dear readers, our responsibilities are different, our positions of service are different, but we all are important to The Lord. Listen, originally from the beginning Adam was the High Priest. Adam was the ruler. Noach was a High Priest. Shem also known as Malki Zedek / King of Righteousness was High Priest. Later the priesthood was the responsibility of the tribal heads. It was because of the failings by the tribal leaders of B'nai Israel at the golden calf incident. That The Lord Separated the tribe of Levi unto Him and the house of Aaron as the Kohanim and Aaron himself as the Kohen Godal.

The tribal leaders {the former priests} had feelings about this matter, yet they understood that the tribe of Levi and the house of Aaron stood out in their righteousness. On the other hand, there were some righteous malcontents, so to speak, in Parshat Korach who were unhappy with The Lord's selections of Moses and Aaron, etc.

So what is the point to all of this? God has not left any of us out. There is a place for each of us!! We may *feel* left out but that is only our perception. We can connect to each other. We can connect to the Torah. We can connect to The Lord. Even though millions of names are not included in the building of the Mishkon, they are not left out. This being the situation, we do not read of anyone feeling left out during the building of the Mishkon. We do not read of contention. We do not hear of ego problems. B'nei Israel was focused on constructing the Mishkon built 100 percent right the first time around. There was a positive attitude that existed.

Rabbi Eli Munk discusses the importance of everyone. He asks,

"Why was a special accounting given for the silver hooks for the pillars {in Exodus 38:28}? Would not one total figure for all the silver used in the Tabernacle have sufficed? According to the Midrash, when Moses initially rendered his accounts to the people, he left out *1,775 shekels* used in making the hooks for the pillars, for they were not visible. It was only after he became concerned that the Israelites might suspect him of wrong doing about the accounts, that with The Lord's help he happened to look at the pillars and was reminded of the hooks.

"This Midrash, explains *Chasam Sofer,* is referring to the fact that although the core of the nation of Israel comprised 600,000 righteous men, there were many worthy Israelites outside of this core, including women, children, and converts {over two and one half million}. Moses was concerned about how he would inspire holiness in those who did not belong to this nucleus {of 600,000}. The Lord then drew his attention to the deeper meaning of the hooks of the pillars, to show him that those who are not part of the core are to be hooked firmly onto the pillars, i.e., to the righteous, who form its inner core.

Vaw Veem, means hooks. The Letter ו Vav appears twice in the word Vaw Veem, *hooks*, and is shaped like a hook; similarly, the Letter ו V*av* often serves as a coordinating conjunction / a connecting letter, in which case it attaches two Words etc.

The hooks signify "EVERYONE IS IMPORTANT." Those in the center of the core, those outside the core and those who are not Jewish. Everyone is important! Yet that does not mean everyone is the same. The hooks also symbolize a future time spoken of by the Novie Zechariah.

Zechariah 8:23

Thus said The Lord, Master of Legions: In those days it will happen that ten men, of all [different] languages of the nations, will take hold, they will take hold of the corner of the garment of a Jewish man, saying, 'Let us go with you, for we have heard God is with you.

Non Jews will take hold of the tzitzit on the corner of a Jewish man's tallit. Zechariah Teaches us that Jews will be clearly distinguished as Jews. Part of that distinguishing factor will be our tallit, our clothing... Non Jews will latch on... will hook on... will connect with the 'RIGHTEOUS JEW.' Many of us have a ways to go to reach that point.... If we continue to try we will eventually get there.

The Gematria for Vaw Vem is 62. This is also the Gematria of Bayn, meaning between.

וָוִים

Vaw Veem – hooks

62 = 40מ 10י 6ו 6ו

בֵּין

Bayn – Divided

62 = 50ן 10י 2ב

Genesis 1:4

'God, divided / separated **between** the light and the darkness...'

Genesis 17:7

'I will establish my covenant **between** Me and you and between your descendants after you throughout their generations for an eternal covenant, to be a God to you, and to *your descendants after you.'*

Exodus 31:12,13

*'B'nei Israel shall guard {preserve} the Sabbath, to maintain the Sabbath for their generations {including the 21st century} as an everlasting covenant***between** *Me and* **between** *B'nei Israel it is an everlasting sign; for in six days The Lord Made the heavens and the earth, and on the seventh day, He abstained from work and He rested.'*

So on one hand Bayn separates between light and dark and on the other hand Bayn connects between The Lord and B'nei Israel.

The Gematria Mispar Godal of Vaw Veem is 622 which is the Gematria for Bih Ree Tee, meaning "Covenant" and also for Ber Chot, meaning blessing. Those of the Covenant who contributed out of the generosity of their heart to the products for the construction of the Mishkon even though they were not of the central core received their special blessing.

Exodus 39:43

'...and Moses Blessed them.'

וָוִים

Vaw Veem – hooks

622 = 600ם 10י 6ו 6ו

בְּרִיתִי

Bih Ree Tee – My Covenant

622 = 10י 400ת 10י 200ר 2ב

בִּרְכַּת

Bee Rih Caht – Blessing

622 = 400ת 20כ 200ר 2ב

The righteous core received their blessing... and

those connected to them received their blessing and those connected to them received their blessing.... etc. {this connection is NOT through intermarriage}

The connection comes from The Lord.

As we complete this time of Parshot study together my prayer is that we each are enriched and will desire to share what we have learned with others and to learn together in another book or course.

Chazak חזך

Be Strong!

Sanctifying Our Communication

Chapter 12

Exodus 30.29

And Separate / Sanctify them and they each shall become [most] Holy of Holies. Anything that touches them will become Holy.

After writing this book I felt like this chapter should conclude our discussion. This is in addition to the Parshat.

We are living in an age that most of us as well as our parents NEVER could have dreamed of. Computers, incredible software, internet, email, cell phones, fiber optics, television screens the size of walls, cable TV, satellite TV, CD's and DVD's, music rumbling from autos a block and a half away and much more. The communications industry is really happening... This communication storm of good and bad raging around us is deteriorating the basic fiber of our long established foundations of Yiddishkeit, God forbid! HOW?

When this book is completed, God Willing it will be available as an e-Book. Who Would have dreamed?

Who has not been impacted by the crashing waves of communication? Consider the reverse of what Rabbi Akiva experienced! As an unlearned shepherd at the age of forty when he stood at the banks of the river observing how seemingly powerful little drops of water falling on hard rock had over time wore away the hard surface of the rock. He used this to motivate himself to become Judaism's greatest scholar. Yet, dear holy reader, unfortunately the reverse is happening to us. The little drops of communication brilliantly landing, splashing and crashing time after time against the foundations of Judaism have begun to take their toll...!! God help us!! IT IS DIFFICULT TO IMAGINE HOW SOMETHING SO WONDERFUL COULD BE SO DAMAGING!

I am NOT by any means suggesting that we rid ourselves of these magnificent tools of communication. However **we MUST learn how to use them properly!!**

At B'nai Noach Torah Institute, LLC we make great efforts NOT to define our religion by Orthodox, Traditional, Conservative, Reform and so forth. We make it a point to replace these defining words with the word "OBSERVANT" understanding that some of us are more or less observant. However in this instance it is necessary to specifically define the problem. All

Jews are impacted by the brilliance of communication. When our conservative, fundamental, hardline right areas of observant Judaism are being impacted, specifically orthodoxy, it weakens *all* of Judaism. It is extremely serious for *all* of Judaism when the foundations of the seriously observant begin to crumble.

For so long the focus has been on intermarriage problems of the less observant.... The focus has been on assimilation... The focus has been on outreach of the observant... the focus has been on the Messianics... be careful of them....

Now, however, the focus is on the breakup of the more seriously observant. WHY?

Fifty years ago few of us had a telephone. Those who did were on a party line. It was expensive to call across town then. Now we have three, four or five phones in our home, caller identification, blocked calls, phone messaging, internet access, etc... Today it costs less to call around the world than it used to cost to call across the state...

Fifty years ago few of us had a television. VCR's, CD's, DVD's, Camcorders did not exist... Now even the more seriously observant have one, two, even three televisions in their home. Few are hidden from sight...

Fifty years ago the computer was an unknown term. Today most American homes, Jewish included, have at least one computer, internet access and games galore...

Dear reader, do not think for one second that these tools of technology have not impacted Judaism. They greatly have. At our Out reach / In reach URL's millions of lessons are studied and the number is growing, thank God...

Yet our first problem is in acknowledging that each of us is impacted by the vastness of the communications industry and that we rely and depend heavily on it. It was only 13 years ago, at the turn of the century / millennium, that everyone was frantic because of our dependence on computers {Y2K}. Our failings are also our blessings... IMMEDIATE ACCESS! It is so readily available.

Most seriously observant Jewish community walls are breached when Jewish families in the community have television and VCR / DVD... If Jewish families have computers with internet access our children find ways to connect with these families. Adults also find ways to connect... Everyone is impacted! TO DENY THIS IS FOOLISH! Parents who brag, "We don't have a television or computer in our home" are only fooling themselves. I have heard so many excuses... 'We only have a monitor in our home... we keep the TV under lock and key... we require passwords to view certain TV programs... our computer denies access to adult sites...'

Kids go to homes that have these connections. Yeshiva boys find where the internet connection is. I see Yeshiva boys in Hotel lobby's, in Hospital lobby's. Who is fooling who? The same holds true for Beis Jacob girls. They find ways to connect when they want to.

Holy reader, this is an attempt to place boundaries on the rotten side of the communications industry. It is an attempt to acknowledge the good and point out the bad! Yet this is only where defining our boundaries begins.

TIME is another factor. TIME is a factor for adults as well as for youth and children. HOW MUCH TIME do we dedicate to any area of communication including the phone? There was a time when Rebbes / Masters – Teachers – Mentors did not have phones in their homes, when Rebbes did not use cell phones. The members of the community had to either visit with the Rebbe at shul or at the Rebbe's home! Visits were frequent and personal. Access was not as immediate as a phone call. Interruptions on the Rebbe's life were more constrained, more controlled than the ringing, clanging, dinging, etc. of a phone. When a person needed to speak to the Rebbe it was a drive or a walk not an easy phone call. Effort was involved! The effort placed a lid on disturbing the Rebbe. NOT SO TODAY!

(Rebbe is a yiddish word derived from the Hebrew Word meaning Rabbi.)

The same can be said for men who talk with each other... for women who talk with each other... for our non adult children who talk with each other...

Dear reader, the time we dedicate to phone usage has an impact on Judaism, on us, on our spouse, on our children, on our Jewish development, on our learning...

One may argue that the phone is a great time saver. There is no denying that. Yet one should think of the phone as a tool. Long ago in the Belk family we made a rule. We do not answer the phone just because it rings. We screen almost every call. We do not return every call. Why? Because our phone is a tool! We use it as a tool! We use our computers in the same fashion.

Holy reader, one must be conscious of the time dedicated to the computer as well as the phone and other communication devices... One should think of their computer / internet access as an instrument also. We receive hundreds of emails each week. Advertisements are deleted without reading! We do not respond to most of our email. Simply put, we cannot reply to all of our email. Many of our emails ask questions we have already discussed and posted on the internet. If the requester did a simple word search they could find the answer on our site. We do respond to pertinent email AS TIME ALLOWS. We use our computer and the internet as a tool!

We could go on and on. All that is required is a little observation to determine how frequently one uses communication devices. The time we spend on these devices, NO MATTER HOW WONDERFUL OR HANDY, must come from somewhere. It is from here that the breakdown occurs, God forbid!

Ladies used to visit the rebbetzin when problems occurred. Now they call. When ladies visited the rebbetzin, she could give attention to the visitors as well as her children. The visitors could also take an active part in attending to needs. When a lady pays a visit to the rebbetzin, there may be other ladies present and sharing on a larger scale can take place. An individual phone conversation does not blend well into the rebbetzin's family life. It isolates the rebbetzin with one person, *robs* time from her children and others who may be present.

Years ago when I was desiring to marry, a dear friend - my Rebbe - arranged for a lady and me to meet and visit at his home one afternoon around a barbeque. We arrived. The Rebbe was in the backyard preparing chicken. The Rebbetzin was on the phone. The Rebbetzin concluded the call after about fifteen minutes. She said it was important. We did not doubt her explanation. Five minutes later another call. This one was also important. Fifteen or twenty minutes passed. The Rebbe excused himself. He went in the house to remind the Rebbetzin that she had guests. A few minutes later she returned. Our barbeque chicken was cool. We ate for a little while. Again the phone rang. Again the Rebbetzin retreated to the house. Thirty minutes later, after numerous apologies by the Rebbe, the lady guest grew weary of waiting and left. I also left, suggesting maybe another time would be better. Dear reader, I have seen this type of thing play out time and time again. It is not necessary to define who was right or wrong in this situation. All that is necessary is to realize that our phone is a tool! If we misuse the tool it is a serious problem.

We could define each communications situation. We could explain blow by blow how they, like little drops of water splash after splash, eventually erode the foundation of the seriously observant families and leaders. That is why it is important to place limits... boundaries on our communication tools...

Now in our parshat this week we

Exodus 30.23 -29

"And spoke The Lord to Moses saying,

'And you, you take top spices, pure myrrh five hundred [shekel weights] and spices of cinnamon from hulf [portions] two-hundred-fifty [shekel weights] and sweet calamus {plant} spices two-hundred-fifty [shekel weights]. And cassia [plant] two-hundred-fifty [shekel weights] in [the] shekel [value of] the Holy [Temple] and 5.7 liters [1 1/2 gallons] of olive oil. Make it into Holy Anointing Oil prepared from the spice blender; a maker of spices. [The blended spice] oil shall be for Holy Anointing. And [then] Anoint the Tent of Meeting, and [Anoint] the Ark of Witness, and [Anoint]

The Table and all Vessels [pertaining to the Table], and [Anoint] the Menorah and all Vessels [pertaining to the Menorah], and [Anoint] the Altar of Incense, and [Anoint] The Altar of Offerings and all the Vessels [pertaining to the Altar of Offerings], [Anoint] The Wash Basin. And [Anoint] The Base [of the Wash Basin]. And Separate / Sanctify them and they each shall become [most] Holy of Holies. Anything that touches them will become Holy.

In other words, anoint and separate everything for The Lord. We read in this passage about the selected spices, the preparation for blending, the expert individual chosen to blend the spices and the purpose for the spices. Now, holy reader, just as great preparation is made to anoint the Holiest Items of the Temple we are required each morning to prepare our vessel.

Part of that preparation is the boundaries that we place on our tools of communication.

If within our home or office we misuse the tools of communication we are in fact disrupting HOLINESS! *i.e.,* we are NOT SEPARATING our tools! If on the other hand we observe proper use of these tools then we are creating holiness. We need to separate everything to The Lord including our communication tools. That is not to suggest that some will not understand why we do not answer the phone or place limits on our phone conversations. It is not to suggest that readers will be pleased with no response to their e-mail...Yet SEPARATION... KEDUSHA is holiness.

Within our neshama... within our home... within our business we must place boundaries on our tools. Our communication tools can be separated. Our communication tools need to be separated so that "anything that touches them will become Holy"... so that we will be instruments of blessing to a world drowning in every form of communication imaginable.

We, the Jewish people, must step forward. We must separate the light and the darkness of communication tools. We must teach our children BY EXAMPLE that it is NOT acceptable to have unlimited phone conversations. Jewish time is precious! Jewish time must be separated wisely to the service of The Lord. We do this to safeguard our homes, our families, our marriages, our mealtimes, our quality of life in Yiddishkeit. Just because a person is a leader or a business owner / manager doesn't mean they have to sacrifice their family life. It is NOT enough to limit our children to the programs, the videos, CD's or DVD's they can watch but the time that they are allowed to spend watching them.

Just as we sanctify time on Sabbath we must sanctify time for The Lord during the rest of the week, sanctify time for our spouses, time for our children, time for our friends, time for ourselves. It is disgusting to observe television being used as a babysitting tool for children. Even when the subject is of the purest and most religious nature. THIS IS A MISUSE OF THE TOOL! PERIOD!! This is not establishing holiness in the sanctity of one's home!! It is NOT teaching our children to properly SEPARATE! It is NOT creating holiness. Everything that touches us or our children or the mezuzah of our home is not being transformed to holiness. Such actions are not transmitting blessing to our children, spouse, neighbors, community or the world.

Some of us are foolish enough to think that our time is unlimited. That is why I highly recommend "EXIT LINES." Exit lines are predetermined lines for both phone, internet and business discussions where one limits their time. Normally it is not acceptable for a person to just walk into one's office / business or home and begin an unscheduled meeting. Such a pattern gives the impression that you have unlimited time. It does not teach separation! If such a situation occurs you can either deny access or limit access. You could say, "I'm sorry but I must prepare for a meeting later today... I cannot discuss this now. Could we reschedule later?" A supervisor normally will appreciate you guarding your time. Other employees will learn your time is valuable. Other people will learn to respect your time and may, in congruence, learn to appreciate the Torah's definition of separation. If the individual is persistent, one might say, "O.K., let's set aside just two or five minutes right now BUT that is the best I can do."

One must guard their time as they guard the

Sabbath! Time is valuable!

In a symbolic way we must anoint all of our communication tools.

What I am saying is not to teach our children or others that all television is wrong or that owning a computer is wrong or having internet access is wrong IS NOT THE PROPER MESSAGE!! These tools of communication and others like them being developed are NOT going away! We must teach separation of good and evil! We must teach proper use of these and other communication tools! In most situations where we prohibit our children and others from using communication tools like phone, television, internet access, etc. we are in fact creating unnecessary RESENTMENT! Just as we teach nidah, kashrut and Sabbath, we must teach the HOLINESS OF COMMUNICATION TOOLS!!

We MUST LEARN to sanctify all the instruments in and around the Mishkon of our lives...

Let's take this to a relationship level. It is NOT acceptable for a husband or a wife to be so wrapped up in whatever they do whereas to neglect their relationship, their children, their relatives or their community.

A Rebbe must set boundaries on the time he spends with his followers. This is what parshat Yitro Teaches. If a Rebbe must do this we likewise must do this. Yitro taught Moses to place boundaries on his access to normal everyday matters. He taught delegation of his responsibilities to other capable individuals. Yitro taught separation of time! A Rebbe like any other husband or parent MUST separate time for his wife and children. I know a Rebbe who practices this like a religion. IT IS A RELIGION! IT IS JUDAISM! He spends quality time with his wife and each of their eleven children. He separates his family from his responsibilities of being a Rebbe. God does not desire a Rebbe or a businessperson to be so involved with what they do to the point of neglect of their spouse, children or relatives... This only leads to the detraction of Yiddishkeit!

Holy reader, we conclude with these Gematrias;

Exodus 30.29

וְקִדַּשְׁתָּ אֹתָם וְהָיוּ קֹדֶשׁ קָדָשִׁים כָּל־
הַנֹּגֵעַ בָּהֶם יִקְדָּשׁ :

כָּל־הַנֹּגֵעַ
Kal - Hah Noh Gay Ah
All touching
ב20 ל30   ה5 נ50 ג3 ע70 = 178

בָּהֶם יִקְדָּשׁ
Baw Hehm - Yeek Dawsh
Will Become Holy
ב2 ה5 מ40   י10 ק100 ד4 ש300 = 461

כָּל־הַנֹּגֵעַ בָּהֶם יִקְדָּשׁ
{All touching these will become Holy}

Total 178 + 461 = 639

This is our goal, that all our instruments within our home and office transmit holiness... including our communication tools!

וְהִתְבָּרְכוּ
Vi Heet Baw Rah Choo {And you will bless}

639= 6ו 20כ 200ר 2ב 400ת 5ה 6ו

The Gematria of both are 639. Think of the place that has the power to transform anything that touches it. This is a very Holy Place. Those who Bless share a relationship to this Holy Place. What does NOT SHARE A RELATIONSHIP to this holy Place? Our tools of communication do not share a relationship with the Holy Place. Why? They are separated from the Holy Place. They are removed. They do not come around the Holy Place! When we add the Gematria for the Lord [26] and the 613 Commands in Ha Torah together we have 639.

Please feel welcome to visit us at:

bnti.us

jewishpath.org

jewishlink.net

7commands.com

Please visit bnti.us/books.html for other books by Dr. Akiva Gamliel Belk.

About The Author

Dr. Akiva Gamliel Belk

Jewish, Husband, Father, Grandfather and Step Great Grandfather.

Graduate:
A.A. Long Beach City College,
B.A. Southern California Bible College,
M.A. Southern California Theological Seminary,
D. Th. Southern California Theological Seminary,
D. Th. Denver Charismatic Theological Seminary

Individual Study:
Rabbi Dovid Nusbaum,
Bais Medrash at Yeshiva Toras Chaim,
Hornosteipler Rebbe, Mordicai Tewerski

Group Study:
Rabbi Yaakov Meyer, Aish Denver
Rabbi Yisroel Engel, Director, Colorado Chabad.

Founder:
Jewishpath.org
Jewishlink.net
7commands.com
Buntings

Dean of Jewish Studies
B'nai Noach Torah Institute, LLC – Biblical Online Studies

Author of various books.
bnti.us/books.html

Businessman:
Realtor and Property Investor

www.ingramcontent.com/pod-product-compliance
Lightning Source LLC
Chambersburg PA
CBHW071723090426
42738CB00009B/1859